Healing the World

Today's Shamans as Difference Makers

HEALING
THE WORLD

SANDRA WADDOCK

Routledge
Taylor & Francis Group

LONDON AND NEW YORK

First published 2017 by Greenleaf Publishing

Published 2017 by Routledge
2 Park Square, Milton Park, Abingdon, Oxon OX14 4RN
711 Third Avenue, New York, NY 10017, USA

Routledge is an imprint of the Taylor & Francis Group, an informa business

British Library Cataloguing in Publication Data:
  A catalogue record for this book is available from the British Library.

    ISBN-13: 978-1-78353-801-0 (hbk)
    ISBN-13: 978-1-78353-772-3 (pbk)

For all who would heal the world.
Especially Malcolm McIntosh. What a gift you are!

Contents

Sandra Waddock is Galligan Chair of Strategy, Carroll School Scholar of Corporate Responsibility, and Professor of Management at Boston College's Carroll School of Management. She has published around 140 papers and 13 books. Recipient of numerous awards, Waddock received the 2016 Lifetime Achievement Award from Humboldt University in Berlin for contributions in corporation sustainability and responsibility, the 2015 award for Leadership in Humanistic Management, and the 2014 Lifetime Achievement Award in Collaboration Research (CSSI Symposium and Partnership Resource Center, Erasmus University), among others. Current research interests are large-systems change, the role of memes in change processes, developing a new narrative for business in society, stewardship of the future, corporate sustainability and responsibility, the problem of growth, wisdom, management education, and intellectual shamans. Her books include *Intellectual Shamans: Management Academics Making a Difference* (Cambridge University Press, 2015), *(Teaching) Managing Mindfully* with Lawrence Lad and Judith Clair (2017), and *Building the Responsible Enterprise: Where Vision and Values Add Value* with Andreas Rasche (Stanford University Press, 2012). Other Greenleaf Publishing books include *SEE Change: Making the Transition to a Sustainable Enterprise Economy* with Malcolm McIntosh (2011) and *The Difference Makers: How Social and Institutional Entrepreneurs Created the Corporate Responsibility Movement* (2008; Social Issues in Management Division Best Book Award, 2011).

Foreword

There is a sentence in Sandra's Waddock's introduction to her enlightened and enlightening book that needs unpacking in the light of events in 2008 and 2016: "We can be, we all are, shamans, and, I firmly believe, all of us want a better world." It is difficult to imagine that everyone doesn't want this, but some days it's difficult. She notes that the word "shaman" originates from the Eastern Siberian Tungus people and means "the person who loves knowledge." Shamans acquire knowledge by being in touch with the spirit world: they are translators of that which lies all around us, but which is difficult for most people, most of the time, to feel. This is especially true in our distraction economy.

While filming a documentary for BBC TV on the Yamal Peninsula in north-east Siberia many decades ago, I was made aware that I, too, could feel the spirit world. I was introduced by my driver, who would not have considered himself to be a shaman, to the spirits in the trees, rocks, and bushes around us. Many of those who practice shamanism as a way of life, or for whom shamanism is as everyday as living and breathing, make sense of a world that many of us—who run from pillar to post excitedly as if we are achieving something—fail to see.

Sensemakers, another word for shamans, are often artists who see round corners and sense the layers upon layers that would open up to us all if we opened our eyes—and our hearts and minds. There has been much talk of late about mindfulness, but I prefer to think of "mindlessness." In this state we let ourselves wander and see what happens. It can take bravery to do this, to lose our inhibitions, and thereby open our minds to wisdom that is not inherent in the distraction economy. "Turn off your mind, relax and float downstream" as John Lennon sang in "Tomorrow Never Knows," drawing on *The Tibetan Book of the Dead*. What goes around . . .

Become a shaman today, yourself, and you will find you will meet others who have also found enlightenment. Light a candle in the darkness and share it with others. But first read this book.

Malcolm McIntosh, PhD, FRSA
With my feet in the hot springs of water that fell
10,000 years ago.
Bath, England, January 2017

Preface

My hope is that this book helps you learn to shine your light in the world. That you become the shaman—the healer, connector, and sensemaker in the service a better world—that you want to be, perhaps that you are meant to be. In this short book, I outline the ways in which today's shaman can work to heal our troubled world, drawing from a rich set of resources about traditional shamanism and, I hope, making the idea of being a shaman in today's world reasonable and accessible for anyone who wants to embark on this journey.

From finding your inner light to healing yourself to healing the world around us. That is the shaman's journey, similar in many respects to what the great mythologist Joseph Campbell called "the hero's quest."[1] It is a universal story, and shamans are found in virtually all parts of the world and cultures. But, today, we do not recognize the shamanic among us, and this book calls for that recognition to arise—and be made explicit. The world, our societies, our business systems, the ecology, and our relationships with each other need all the healing that a shaman can give, all the connecting across the numerous divides we face, and all the sensemaking that is possible to help all of us shape a better world together.

Shamans, I argue, act in all domains and any number of ways. Whatever your calling and purpose in life, there is a way that you can tap your inner shaman and begin your path of healing—self, other, and the world. To do that, we all have to, in a sense, die to the old ways and welcome the new. We need to find balance and create harmony where they seem not to exist now. We can draw on science to help us in this task and know that perhaps we who would be healers are not so strange, after all. We can apply, as I do towards the end of the book, these ideas in the context of today's business and economic systems. We can envision a better world for all, where "all" includes not just us humans but also other living beings and nature herself.

We can be, we all are, shamans and, I firmly believe, all of us want a better world.

Acknowledgments

No book belongs solely to the author. In this case, this book "belongs," in a sense, to the wonderful *Intellectual Shamans* and *Difference Makers* I've written about earlier,[2] who helped me understand how they operate as shamans, healers, and difference makers in our world. It belongs to all the colleagues with whom I have written about corporate responsibility, business in society, management education, multi-sector collaboration, large system change, and leading for wellbeing, among so many other topics, over many years. It belongs to all of those scholars, writers, teachers, and students from whom I have learned so much, and whose wisdom I can only aspire to gain. It belongs to colleagues, friends, and family and all of those who understand who I am and love me anyway. It belongs to the Way of Power group which has helped me to articulate these ideas. It belongs to my many musician friends and fellow songwriters whose grace, spirit, and insights lead and inspire in a different way. It belongs to Alan, whose humor keeps me humble and whose stability and love keep me grounded, and to my son, Ben Wiegner, whose humor and grace light up my life. I am grateful to all of you, I love all of you, too many to name without overlooking someone important, but you know who you are.

Note: Some parts of this book were published in blog form on one of my websites prior to being consolidated into this book.

Sandra Waddock
Boston, January 2017

1

Healing the world: why shamanism?

> Wherever you stand, be the soul of that place.
>
> Rumi

What does it mean to be or become a shaman today? And how can being shaman today help to heal our troubled world: that is, make the world a better place? Shamans are known as healers in traditional cultures—medicine men and women. For many of us, the idea of shamanism is linked to the myths and practices of traditional cultures that do not necessarily align with our times, cultures, and needs. *Healing the World: How Today's Shamans Can Make the World a Better Place* puts shamans—the healers, connectors, and sensemakers who wish to use their particular gifts to make the world a better place[3]—explicitly into today's context. Our world is fraught with problems that demand the best healing attention we each can provide in our own ways in becoming shamans: problems such as sustainability crises, climate change, political divisiveness, economic, energy, security, and food uncertainty, terrorism, poverty, injustice, lack of jobs, and failing institutions, to name only a few, some of which threaten the very future of humanity on the planet.

In this context, the world, our beautiful green Earth, the living planet called Gaia,[4] needs many more of us to become and be shamans—healers of our troubled world, so our relationships in and to the world can be healed. We humans need to learn to treat each other and the world around us with the dignity that they deserve. We need to heal our relationship with planet Earth, conceived as Gaia, so she can continue to support the human enterprise. As shamans, the healers of relationships of all sorts,[5] we need to heal our relationships with other people, other living beings, and nature herself. We need to heal our political and economic systems so they support and enhance life in all its aspects. Only then can we all learn to flourish in this world together as one human species deeply interconnected with all other living beings and with Gaia.

This book unpacks what it means to *become* and *be* a shaman today in terms that that informed readers can understand and relate to with our scientific, rationalistic, and "realistic" mind-sets. *Healing the World* attempts to take the fundamentals of shamanism and translate them for anyone interested in playing the important healing role of the shaman today, particularly in the larger context of our communities, businesses, and other institutions, many of which are in trouble and desperately need the healing touch of the shaman.

In some ways, this book tells my story, both intellectually and personally. The book, though, is meant to be much more than one person's story: it is really about how you—anyone—with the will and a commitment to healing the part of the world that you impact can take on the mantle of the shaman—the healer, connector, and sensemaker in the service of a better world. Here I argue that you can do so without the trappings of shamanism as it is known and understood in many traditional societies. That is, we can translate the work of the shaman for today's world and today's problems. *Healing the World* is about shamanism in today's context, what it means, how it plays out, who can do it, and why it matters.

Today's shaman

What is today's shamanism? Basically, shamanism describes experiences that are out of the realm of everyday, concrete, and empirically observable reality. Shamanism today is about using your gifts and abilities of healing, connecting, and sensemaking to make a positive difference in the world.

If you are skeptical about things like shamanism, as I am, you might already be saying: OK, now you're getting weird. Though consider: Have you ever walked into a room and sensed the energy of that room? Had an intuition? A strong hunch? A sudden "knowing"? A creative impulse that just "hits" you? Where *does* the artist get his inspiration, the songwriter and composer her muse, the dancer the understanding of what moves make sense in this particular situation? Where does the creative impulse that puts two ideas together in new ways come from? How does the change agent know where the leverage points are that result in change in a desired direction? How does the therapist know what question or insight will cause the patient to see things differently and be able to act differently? Or the doctor know that this and not that is the right diagnosis or what is the right treatment for *this* patient? How does the nurse know what words or healing techniques will comfort a patient in distress?

Think about it. These and many other "ordinary" experiences are really extraordinary. They do not come from logical trains of thought. We call them brainstorms, intuitions, hunches, and insights. We cannot analyze, rationalize, or deduce our way to them. Scientific explanations are lacking in providing understanding about how they arise. Instead, they draw from some inner source, some place of wisdom, some connection made intuitively, from Spirit or something beyond yourself—call it what you will. That something inspires, gives insight and direction, and helps us find the path to healing, creativity, connection, or sensemaking inherent in the particular situation we are facing.

There are many ways in which such experiences happen. For example, deep concentration about a problem, dreaming, questioning, and thinking where we "lose" ourselves can open us to such insights or experiences. Meditations of all forms, trance states induced in any number of ways. Hypnosis, getting into the "zone" or the state of "flow" where time disappears and all is focused on the task at hand. Really connecting with another person, team, or group in this moment. Focused attention to accomplish something that seemed difficult or impossible. All of these experiences take us out of everyday reality and into the shamanic state, at least briefly. All of them require focus, concentration, *attention* to something beyond ourselves and a willingness to take what we are "given" and use it appropriately.

In a sense, such experiences require us opening ourselves to what needs to—or might—come, if we simply let it. I call this latter skill "allowing," allowing what wants to come to life to do so, whether it is a creative impulse, a sudden recognition, a connection, or something else than brings a new perspective. "Allowing" involves recognizing that what needs to be is already there if we just get out of its way and "allow" it to come. Doing that, though, takes work, letting go of fear, and willingness to recognize when the extraordinary is happening.

Most if not all of us have these types of unexplainable creative surges, sudden insights, connections, and intuitions. The difference between the shaman and the rest of us is that the shaman recognizes and uses them in constructive ways. The shaman does not dismiss them or their potential power. The shaman knows when and how to act on them for the greater good of self, other, community, and even the world. It is the desire to develop the awareness, insight, and courage to open up to the "magic" of such experiences and the acceptance of the gift that they are to us that moves us towards being shaman.

Essentially, I believe that we each in our own ways can take on the sacred, even spiritual (albeit not religious in the denominational sense), task of healing those parts of the world where our powers reach. We can accomplish this task through our relationships, our work, our creativity, our insights. Healing is the core task of the shaman. Shamanism, in this sense, is about facing a troubled world (or person or community) and finding ways to explain it and help it heal. It is about realizing that human civilization has to go beyond survival to thriving in the future. Each of us must do our bit to heal what is wrong in our world. In such a troubled world, there is no standing on the sidelines. There needs to be a holistic and realistic recognition of the nature of the world's problems, where we can each find a leverage point from which change can begin. That is the healing task of today's shaman. Shamanism in this sense is about power, our own power, discovering and using that power for the good of people and the world around us.

Fundamentally, then, this book is about my belief that, in our troubled world, many more of us from the typically secular world need to take on that healing mantle of the shaman, despite the apparent strangeness or weirdness (*wyrdness* in its original sense of pertaining to personal destiny) of the term. Even those of us who decry the strangeness inherent in traditional approaches to shamanism can, I believe, tap into our own shamanic resources. The modern shaman does not necessarily need, in my view, to rely on ritual and ceremony. She or he does not even need to have the vivid imaginal life that allows him or her to see and connect with power animals and spirits of various sorts. We do not need to be called to "new age" spirituality or to traditional versions of shamanism to undertake the tasks of healing, connecting, and sensemaking associated with the shaman.

The word "shaman" comes from the Tungus tribe of eastern Siberia.[6] A direct translation of the word "shaman" from the Tungus-Manchzhur language is "a person who loves knowledge." "Sham" in that language means knowledge, and "man" means "liker," therefore "shaman" means "lover of knowledge."[7] As the historian and philosopher Mircea Eliade notes in his comprehensive book *Shamanism*, practices associated with shamans can be found in a wide variety of forms in most traditional cultures of the world.[8]

The term "shaman" and the work of the shaman needs to be brought into everyday use, so that many more people can deliberately and explicitly play the important role of healer for our troubled world. Coming from a management professor in a fairly conservative research institution, this call for many more of us to become shamans may seem unusual. I am, however, increasingly convinced of the need for more healers of all sorts and in all areas of work in our world, people to take on this work explicitly and deliberately. I am also convinced that anyone with the will and right intent can do this work—and it need not be imbued with mythology, ritual, and the kinds of trappings that put some people off. In my view, shamanism means accepting your experiences beyond ordinary reality, your powers of healing, connecting, and sensemaking. Shamanism means finding and accepting your deepest and most central source of power. Then it means using that power to do something good for the world around you, as that "something good" suits your interests and your gifts.

The work of the shaman

Traditional shamans' work is frequently grounded in local mythologies, mysteries, and practices, complete with sometimes arcane rituals and use of various techniques and substances for achieving the trance state that permits new information and insights to be gleaned. Unlike traditional and Indigenous shamans, my work as a shaman (to the extent that I can call myself shaman) is grounded in the modern world and in efforts to "test" what works and does not (though such testing is not always possible to the extent that would satisfy me). Like my own teacher, John Myerson, I attempt to present this information without calling upon lots of rituals or arcane practices that, which though helpful to traditional shamans in their particular contexts, do not necessarily always appeal to the modern sensibility. Like the academic that I am at heart, I remain skeptical about much of shamanism—even as I passionately believe that we can all become shamanic if we wish and use what can only be called the power that is associated with shamanism for good.

The shaman is the healer in traditional cultures: the medicine man or woman. The shaman has three main roles: healer, connector, and sensemaker, used in the service of a better (healed) world, community, or person. As healer, the shaman is responsible for the wellbeing of the individual patient or the whole community. Healing often is believed to result from the shaman's collecting information from different (spiritual) realms or making new connections in his or her connector role. Then the shaman brings that information back to the community in the sensemaking capacity to heal what is wrong by creating new narratives or telling new stories that heal what is broken in the local mythologies. These tasks of the shaman will be explored in more depth later on.

Here I want to note that, in attempting to modernize the concept of shamanism to today's healers, connectors, and sensemakers, I honor traditional understandings of the shaman, while still arguing for that adaptation to *today's* culture and times. Each shamanic tradition arose in a particular context and is suited to that context. Taking the mythologies, rituals, and ceremonies of different cultures and using them in a different context, however, does not always create a meaningful way for people to relate to those ideas. Importantly, it is the *idea* of the shaman as healer of the world around us, I believe, not the particular trappings, beliefs, or identities that go with any particular manifestation of shamanism, that truly matters. It is this idea that we can all be or become healers of our world, become shamans for our times and places, that I believe is central to today's shaman.

Shamanism itself has always adapted to and arisen out of particular contexts, and so today's shamanism can adapt to today's needs, circumstances, and places. Today's shamans are the shapers of our mythologies and beliefs, they are the healers that we turn to, they are our most impressive and substantive leaders and artists, and, as I will try to illustrate later, can be found in any walk of life. They are among us if we can learn to see and appreciate them. They can *be* us if we have the will, the courage, and the desire to become them.

Some might want to accuse me or this project of cultural appropriation in translating the idea of the shaman to our times. Cultural appropriation means taking others' ideas or practices and using them as your own. The reality is, however, that shamans are found in virtually all cultures, including our own. We just don't often recognize them in our mainstream way of life. The project here is to raise up today's shamans and make their work visible so that others, drawing on our own cultural resources, can become shamans in their own right, without necessarily resorting to practices better suited to other cultures. Indeed, my own training has provided little in the way of ritual that draws on Indigenous cultures, and I do not believe that such ritual is necessary for us to be able to tap our own gifts and powers of healing. So do not expect magic, mysticism, or ritualistic techniques that guide you to spirits, power animals, or other guides, unless such approaches make sense to you and you develop them on your own (which, by the way, is entirely feasible).

Here, then, is the premise that I am working with: We are all shamans, or we can be. At least, if we desire to and do the work, we all have the potential to become shamans, though the path is not always easy and there is certainly some risk involved. Fur-

ther, there is power in shamanism, though in becoming a shaman that power is different from what we typically think of as
power. Shamanic power does not have much to do with posi-
tional authority or wealth. Rather, it has to do with the intent to
heal and purpose that moves your work in the direction of healing. This belief comes from my own experience of working in a
shamanic group for nearly 15 years. It also comes from a study
of a group of academics I call "intellectual shamans," and from
a wide range of reading about shamans in other cultures and
today.[9] It comes also from work on a group of individuals I call
"difference makers," who have steadily worked for many years
to build an infrastructure that holds businesses accountable for
their impacts—and in that way do their own shamanic healing
work.[10]

The shaman uses healing, connecting (or boundary-spanning),
and sensemaking to help create a better world by healing something. The core of shamanism is the healing function. Shamans
in our modern world have a passion for in some way making the
world a better place. Shamans have, in a sense, a gift that they
can use in the service of healing. It took me years to recognize
that I have any shamanic gifts at all because mine are not the
traditional shaman's gifts of seeing into other realms, having
spiritual experiences of various sorts, or even explicitly healing
people. What I finally realized is that we all have *different* gifts
that we can use in bringing out our own shamanic tendencies.
What I can do is different from what you can do shamanically.
We will go into more detail on these ideas later.

Though shamanism is fundamentally about healing, it is also
about power and spirit. Shamans do have a certain power,
because they access information—knowledge and sometimes
wisdom—that others may not yet be able to access. They can

use that information for healing, connecting, and sensemaking purposes, and they also use it, in a sense, to heal themselves before they can begin to heal others. Part of the sense of power resides in self-confidence while other parts are linked to insight, courage, and risk-taking for healing purposes.

Shamanism: the world's oldest spiritual tradition

Shamanism is thought to be the world's oldest and perhaps most widespread spiritual tradition. Shamans can be found in all parts of the world and in virtually every traditional culture. If we think of the shaman as primarily a healer, whether of physical bodies, souls, cultural mythologies, and cultures themselves at whatever level they appear, as some scholars do, then we begin to understand the pervasiveness of shamanism. Indeed, Mircea Eliade's classic book, published in 1951, explored the idea of the shaman in cultures around the world, particularly focusing on uses of trance and ecstasy as core experiences and ways of accessing spirits, different realms, and new information.[11] Eliade's book, which is still considered a foundational and seminal work on shamanism, documents the pervasiveness of the concept of the shaman across cultures globally, though sometimes the shaman is known by other names, such as medicine man or woman. Eliade also documents the many ritualistic and ceremonial practices and belief systems associated with traditional shamanism.

As noted earlier, the term "shaman" is thought to come from the Tungus tribe in what is now Siberia, and is possibly over 2,000 years old. Shamanism as described by Eliade was defined as a "technique of religious ecstasy." The term broadly refers to (mostly Indigenous) spiritual and healing practices that attempt to bring harmony and balance to man, nature, and communities. Ecstasy, as used by Eliade, means going into a trance state to transcend normal consciousness and the barriers that it imposes. In this trance state or state of altered consciousness, the shaman is able to "see" (feel or experience) new information needed for healing purposes. This state is what I call non-ordinary experience—the state where insights come, however attained.

Because traditional shamans are believed to be communicating with spiritual beings, and because many traditional cultures believe that magic is involved in such communications, there are spiritual and religious overtones to most concepts of shamanism. Thus, shamanism is known as the world's oldest spiritual tradition. More generally, shamanism can be considered to be a way of connecting with nature and natural processes, with other people or creatures, or across various boundaries, as in seeking inspiration and insight. As I will explore later in more depth, I believe that the shamanic trance state is a way of connecting with what psychologist Carl Jung called the collective unconscious, and it is from that source that insights come.[12] Shamanism is a process that, when used well, evokes wisdom among its practitioners, as well as a healing orientation aimed at balance and harmony in all relationships, including the relationship that you have with yourself.

While I am using the term "shaman" in a more secular sense than in many traditions, it is important to acknowledge the spiritual heritage of the term. Shamanism is not a religion in the traditional sense, although particular cultures do have a wide range of belief systems associated with their shamanic practices;

thus, within some specific cultures, shamanism can be seen as a religion or certainly a form of spirituality. Mostly, shamanism is associated with spirituality in that shamanic practitioners attempt to travel or "journey" to other (spiritual) realms to commune with (spiritual) entities to gather information that can help the local community.

Let me briefly differentiate between spirituality and religion as I understand it. Here the term "spirituality" is used to designate some sort of connection with something "greater than." In effect, spirituality is a search for something in life that is bigger than ourselves, whether we call that thing a higher being, god, the collective unconscious, the "universe," purpose, meaning, or something else. Generally, spirituality has the connotation of seeking meaning in life, searching for the sacred, or going inward to find what is important to a particular person. Many people today understand spirituality in terms of personal growth and transformation as they explore the world about them, their inner world, and what life means to them. For many people, their spirituality is expressed through a particular religion, but spirituality need not be associated with a specific religion—or religion at all.

Religion is a more specific belief in or worship of a particular "greater than" power, God, or gods. Religion is generally associated with a set of beliefs or faith, particular practices, behaviors, and worldviews. Religions often identify God or gods, along with other spiritual beings, in which their adherents believe, and whose dictates and precepts help guide their adherents' lives. Obviously, there are many religions in the world, each of which has its own set of beliefs and practices, with Christianity, Islam, Hinduism, and Buddhism forming the largest sects. Shamans in traditional cultures can and do adhere to particular culturally relevant sets of beliefs and practices as well, so, in some cases, shamanism has many of the trappings of religion. Importantly, though, you can become and be a shaman in the context of any set of religious beliefs you might hold.

Shamanism today needs to be understood as a means of making the world a better place. That is, being a shaman means serving some sort of larger purpose or creating some sense of meaning and purpose in ways that are set in the context of or go beyond any particular culture or set of traditions, practices, and beliefs. At the same time, any specific way of engaging with the tasks of the shaman in serving the world needs to be grounded in the particular culture and myths of the individual shaman so that the shaman can relate to the community.

Because shamanic practice frequently involves shifting the cultural mythologies that constitute how a given community conceives itself, the shaman represents and makes sense of the ways that people in a given community perceive and relate to the world around them. For example, a local traditional mythology might involve myths, ideas, and tales about what humans' roles in the world are *vis-à-vis* spiritual beings' roles. It might involve how people interact with other "beings," including spirit beings. Local cultural myths might explain how a given community thinks that world came into being in the first place, i.e., an origin myth. Or the myth could describe how people believe that their world operates today, especially with respect to the spirits and souls that inform the culture. The myth could explore how people should act towards each other and towards nature. Shamanic practices in traditional cultures include numerous rituals and practices that embody a particular culture's beliefs and help the shaman relate, through the local mythology, to the person who is suffering.

Interestingly, in our modern era, one of the most dominant cultural mythologies is that of science, i.e., that we can and should know what we know only through the tenets of science, i.e., through scientific exploration and empirical findings. Another myth of the developed world is that man [*sic*] is separate from nature and can (and should) attempt to control nature (despite evidence that such control simply is not possible, nor are we actually separate from nature). Another core set of beliefs that affect many in the developed world, almost as religion in some quarter, involves the roles and activities of businesses and economies. In this story or narrative, economies and businesses are supposedly oriented toward constant growth, "free" markets, consumers as the basic social being, laissez-faire governments, and individualism, especially in the United States. We will explore these myths in greater detail later.

Grounding shamanism for today

Key to understanding shamanism in the modern (or any) context is that it deals with imbalances of various sorts—in the patient, in a community, in the world, in humans' relationships with the world around us, with each other, or with other living beings. The healing done by the shaman is all about bringing balance back into relationships that exist within the self, between the self and others, and between the self and nature or the world. The shaman's work is to somehow bring the world or community, which is dis-eased or dis-ordered, back into order. Since we all know people who undertake these tasks in various ways and numerous occupations, creative work, and activities, it relatively easy to see that it is possible to be a shaman doing virtually any type of work.

Let me explain a bit more about this conception of today's shaman. In my book *Intellectual Shamans*, I studied a group of management academics whose work has elements of shamanism, i.e., the healing, connecting, and sensemaking orientations that are common to all shamans. Before this book, these individuals would almost surely not have identified themselves as shamans, though they did not object when I did so. But their work, which is aimed at healing their disciplines, their theories and ideas, the practice of management, approaches to research and teaching, among other things, carries distinct aspects of shamanism set in today's context. They approach their work with a healing orientation, attempting to heal their discipline or its practices. They connect across boundaries, frequently disciplinary, sector, research-practice, or theory-teaching boundaries, to gather new insights and information just as traditional shamans cross into spiritual realms from our day-to-day realm of activities. Finally, because they have become leaders in their various fields, they have the bully pulpit to become sensemakers through their writing, speaking, consulting, and teaching for other people. That is, intellectual shamans can be thought leaders or even public intellectuals, reframing ideas, generating new ideas and insights, and pulling together existing ideas in new ways. They often make sense out of the linkages of ideas that others have not yet seen.

In the next chapter, we will explore more about who today's shamans are. In the rest of the book, we will explore what it means to be a shaman today. Since the existence of shamans goes back thousands of years, there have already been efforts have been made to bring the idea of the shaman into our times.

Here I will try to do so without the trapping of mysticism that typically surround such efforts. In taking on this task, I hope to show that the shaman in modern times is the person who is willing to take the initiative, risk, and effort to make this world a better place—for ourselves, our children, and for all who will follow those children. That person can be in virtually any walk of life. There are, however, certain characteristics that probably need to be present to ensure that the work and the world of the shaman are kept sacred. This sacredness exists because the work of shaman needs to be approached with reverence and respect, even though I have defined the practice as secular in the sense of not being affiliated with any particular religious or spiritual tradition. As we will see, shamanism today is sacred because of its holistic sense of trying to make this world a better place for all.

2

Shamans: world healers among us

Shamans walk among us all the time. They are the people you think of as visionaries, seers, or, as my cousin says, people who see around corners. Sometimes they seem to anticipate what is going to happen, make connections others don't make, link people together who need to meet, have great instincts, or stand out in other ways. They may be the artists whose painting makes you feel more deeply or seems to reflect our times or the future in ways that others do not, or the songwriters and musicians whose music allows access to hidden emotions and thoughts. They may be writers or poets whose ideas inspire or give insights you might have otherwise missed. They may be counselors who get you to open up about issues that have been troubling you but could not be healed until they were acknowledged.

Modern shamans can be teachers or parents who seem to work magic with children, understanding and guiding them towards healthy, productive lives. They are the physicians, nurses, therapists, and technicians who connect in real ways with their patients and help guide them towards a healing way of life … or safely guide them to make the transition to the world beyond when that is necessary. They are the firefighters, police officers, assembly-line workers, managers, waitstaff, and clerks who brighten the day when you interact with them, and help to make the world seem like a better place. They are the grandmothers and grandfathers, aunts, uncles, brothers, and sisters whose words soothe or make sense when we are troubled or excite when we need encouragement. They are healers, connector, and sensemakers who stimulate us to be our best selves and do their bit to make the world a better place.

Some modern shamans operate explicitly in a healing profession, using energy, intuition, and insight, along with their expertise, knowledge, and learned skills, of course, to help others. Some are activists, focused on improving the community, society, or natural world around us by using their own inner light to help guide others to productive and healing decisions for that world. Sometimes they are leaders, business people, politicians, spiritual leaders, workers and leaders in non-profit and non-governmental organizations (NGOs), and community organizers who can inspire others. I imagine that we all could say that we all know people in a wide range of occupations and activities who undertake similar challenges. These people work to heal people, communities, and the world, crossing normal boundaries to find new ideas, helping us make sense out of those ideas—healing, connecting, and sensemaking.

If the three central tasks of the shaman— , healing, connecting, and sensemaking—are indeed the core of shamanic practice, then arguably we can each identify doctors, nurses, psychotherapists of all sorts, spiritual leaders, village soothsayers, wise elders, artists in all media, therapists, poets, dancers, musicians,

entrepreneurs, visionaries, inventors, clerks, workers in factories, farmers, reporters, actors, leaders, priests, ministers, rab-
bis, pandits, imams, and ayatollahs, entrepreneurs and social
entrepreneurs, and leaders of many business enterprises, especially social enterprises, plus government officials, members of
NGOs and non-profit enterprises, volunteers, social and civic
activists—or simply difference makers, as possible shamans who
want the world to be a better place. Further, we all know friends
and family members who relate to people in healing ways. They
may listen in a special way and offer their restorative energy and
insights, and help us to connect to ourselves, to each other, to a
higher power. Generally, they help make sense of the world in
new ways. All of these people can, in their own ways, be considered to be undertaking a form of shamanic practice when they
incorporate healing, connecting, and sensemaking into their
work and activities—in the service of a better world, or, less
grandly, of helping someone else.

Sometimes today's shamans are social or conventional entrepreneurs who want to make the world a better place by bringing
their ideas into a new enterprise, the work of which enhances
lives, improves nature, or builds new connections in societies.
Some work in businesses or other institutions, walking the interstices between business-as-usual's currently harmful trajectory
and creating change that moves the enterprise toward account-
ability, responsibility, transparency, and sustainability. Maybe
they are governmental officials or politicians, who think holistically and systemically about the issues facing their constituents
and communities. They may work to improve those conditions,
connecting across socio-economic, racial, ethnic, and religious
divides, bringing people together to work for the good of the
whole.

I am very lucky: I know lots of folks that I would classify as having at least some of the power of the shaman, whether they know it or not, and whether they have explicitly developed it or not. Some of these people are "difference makers,"[13] i.e., social and institutional entrepreneurs, and "intellectual shamans," i.e., academics who attempt to integrate across disciplines, theory and practice or teaching to serve the world. Others are activists, scholars, and leaders in business, communities, schools, and civil society enterprises.

Shamans are the people of light, as I'll discuss in the next section. Shamans think holistically and are imbued with a sense of purpose or mission that involves making the world around them a better place. In businesses and other enterprises, the people who tend toward the shamanic are the boundary-spanners and change agents who walk and work in multiple worlds or contexts at once, and who often serve in the role of translator between those worlds. They are the social entrepreneurs, who try to mix social mission with balanced or profitable financial statements, trying to do good in the world by bringing together two different sets of values. They are the activists who cross multiple boundaries in their efforts to make a difference, who can "hold" the inherent tensions, contradictions, and even paradoxes of their different spheres of activity simultaneously.

Is everyone who does these things shamanic? No, and certainly they would not all think of themselves as shamans. But could it be that these people are somewhere along that healing path? Could it be that with some support and understanding they could broaden their reach, in a sense, their power to transform themselves and others in positive ways?

People of light

If you look into the eyes of a shaman, you'll likely see a kind of light. Or perhaps you will see or feel this light emanating from the heart. Perhaps that person seems to "electrify" the room when she or he enters, drawing people to him or her. Shamanism in a sense is about energy—and this "light" is a form of energy that seems to exude from some people. A friend of mine, Professor James P. Walsh of the University of Michigan, says that he is always attracted to people who have this light. Indeed, it is by this light that shamans often recognize each other. You can see this light in a lot of people who would not necessarily identify as shamans, but whose work and practices may lead them along the healing path of the shaman.

Walsh, as quoted in my book *Intellectual Shamans*,[14] says explicitly that this light that comes from certain people is a source of inspiration, "I am very aware of the people I keep around me," says Walsh. "I try to keep the company of people who have that some kind of special quality. They're authentic, they're genuine, and they've got passion. Sure, they're smart and all of that, but there's something real about them. You get this palpable sense of something else. You can feel it. I can't really articulate it, but it's there . . . I think of them as having a light that shines from them. These people inspire me to find that same kind of light in myself, to honor who I am, honor the moment, and essentially ask me to aim higher and reach farther."

Think of those people you know who seem to light up the room when they enter. Maybe it is their smile or sense of humor. Maybe it is their particular way of connecting with other people. Maybe it is the light in their eyes that speaks of joy and passion or the way they pay attention to you and others. Maybe it is their engagement and passion about what it is that they're doing, whether that is speaking, doing business, creating a work of art or literature, or simply just "being," in the sense of being present to what is happening in the moment. Their appeal is certainly not just about looks or the way they dress. It's got a lot more to do with inner than outer beauty.

What *is* that light that is shining through?

It could be happiness. It could be a sense of personal wellbeing, a kind of contentment with the self, with life, and with things just as they are. That type of presence is often found in people who have practiced mindfulness techniques, of which there are a multitude, over a period of time. It could be something bigger than the person, a sense of broader purpose that lights up the person's eyes. It could be related to the joy of giving to others, rather than simply acquiring whatever might be considered important for one's self, e.g., power, money, material objects like houses, cars, and the latest gadgets. It could be that the person is drawing from a wellspring of creativity that comes from building, writing, knitting, speaking, drawing, painting, making music, woodworking, or some other creative pursuit that brings beauty into the world. It could come from helping at a food kitchen, building homes or furniture for others, the community or barn raising, the artistry of cooking healthful and beautifully displayed food to share with others, working in a garden, or walking out in nature. It could come from any number of other things that help ground these people of light, help them share their particular gifts with others, or bring something new and interesting into the world.

What is this light? Of course, it's impossible to know for sure. It may have something to do with purpose, self-awareness, confidence, and knowing your place in the world, which gets reflected in a form of energy that exudes from people of light. It comes, I think, from a sense of feeling and being "whole," complete, even when they recognize their own imperfections and flaws. I suppose we could call it authenticity combined with positive purpose. There is a reason that we call some people of light "enlightened." There is a reason that wisdom "illuminates" or makes things "clear."

Such enlightenment goes along with some inner sense that you are doing the work you need to do, you are fulfilling your bigger purpose in the world, in whatever form that purpose takes. It can mean that you have become fully who you need to be or are. It could mean that you have discovered and actually like the person you are and in some sense the person you must be. It may also have to do with the direct connection with spirit, the universe, the One, a higher purpose or calling, God, by whatever name you call it, which shamanic practice enables. The shaman achieves enlightenment by becoming, in a sense, one with self, with other, with the world, and with the universe—much as Buddhist philosophers have told us is possible through extensive meditations and related practices.

Light, of course, is a form of energy and it is energy that shamans work with, since, in a quantum sense, all is energy. The inner light that shamans seem to have may come from their connection to source (universe, spirit, God, or whatever you call it). Or it may come from the deep curiosity and desire to help others and the world, or from their ability to "see" what others find hard to see. In speaking about intellectual shamans, I described this light as coming from seemingly boundless intellectual curiosity and a willingness to take risks which also provide rewards in terms of insights, ideas, and new connections. It is expressed in excitement about ideas, for the intellectual shamans, or for others perhaps in excitement about art, connecting with other people, doing work or activities you love, caring for people, or whatever it is that centers, guides, and inspires. In a sense, intellectual and other shamans are on a quest to make the world a better place and, as they try to make sense of what they are learning, they link their inner light and energy with wisdom, with knowing themselves, and with a sense of peace, place, and purpose in the world. Shamans know and understand the transformative power available in the proper use and direction of their inner energy towards healing purposes. That energy is at least part of what I believe creates the light that draws people to shamans.

The inner light of the shaman may also come from the fact that the shaman tends to follow what we can call his or her own "lights," rather than allowing the dictates of society, hierarchy, parents, religion, or others to rule. Often, shamans are a bit "outside" what might be called the normal path. The intellectual shamans that I studied, for example, were frequently mavericks, having following their own intellectual lights over the years, sometimes at considerable risk to their careers, although, at least for the people I studied, ultimately achieving success. But their career paths were not always straight and narrow, though sometimes they were. It was their intellectual, scholarly, and work paths that took them on different routes from the norm. Sometimes, though not always, they found themselves doing considerable wandering around before they found a way forward that allowed their own inner lights to shine. Today's shamans may not always fit in to narrowly conceived or constrained systems or their structures neatly, because in following their own lights, they are carving out paths seldom traveled by others.

There is satisfaction in following one's own inner light rather than that of others or of living the life that others want for you, rather than what you are "meant" to do. Living by your own light entails a degree of risk because it can mean sometimes stepping outside the boundaries of what others' expectations might be.

Doing so allows the shaman to do what is needed to make connections with self, with others, with the community or system, and with whatever universal power or spirits are calling. Following the inner light can create a sort of magnetism for that person to which others are attracted, which may be the source of what is called a "strange attractor" in chaos theory. For example, the intellectual shamans are some of those people to whom others are attracted: for example, at a conference or meeting where they might be speaking, or to their books, blogs, and articles when they publish.

The light that shamans have can thus be compared to what physicists call the "strange attractor," when speaking about how a semblance of order comes out of fractal structures in chaotic systems. The idea of the strange attractor was initially discussed by MIT meteorological researcher Edward Lorenz in the 1960s without specifically using the term, which was later coined by physicists David Ruelle and Floris Takens to describe the dynamics of turbulence.[15] A strange attractor is a kind of focal point around which a pattern emerges in a chaotic system: that is, it is something around which other parts of the system evolve because it seems to "attract" those elements into different configurations. Similarly, the shaman is often an attractive figure within his or her community, creating a focal point for healing but also for relationships, community, and various types of healing and other work that needs to get done. Some shamans attract and connect ideas or artistic insights. Others attract activism and resources to get things done. Still others focus on attracting whatever they need for healing purposes relevant to their particular work or interests. Between the light that the shaman exudes and the nature of his or her work, particularly in healing relationships of all sorts, the reason for serving as an attractor becomes clear.

Because the shaman plays a role in bringing about order from dis-order and ease from dis-ease, their work also sheds a kind of light on the world. Healing brings new light—life—to the person, organization, system, or community that has been troubled. Connecting brings the light of insight to ideas, people, and systems that need to be connected in some way. When they use their sensemaking skills, shamans also help to illuminate and clarify the world for others in new ways by generating new memes or core phrases, images, and other types of artifacts that help define a system, telling new stories or creating new narratives that help people understand their world better, or otherwise making sense of the world around them. Allowing the inner light to shine is clearly important to the way of the shaman in part because sometimes there are significant risks during the early phases of shamanic practice that must be taken as one heeds the call to shamanism. Those risks can be career risks that place the emerging shaman outside the mainstream of whatever field she or he is in; they can be visionary ideas that seem unrealistic or unusual; they can be new types of enterprises or organizations or ways of doing things that people do not recognize— or any number of other types of risks. That said, the light that shines from shamans suggests that the risks are well worth taking.

I knew someone who shined from an inner light. She exuded joy in every interaction she had. She was a scholar, a researcher, an academic, who brought new ideas to life through her work. But she was far more than that. You would never know that she struggled for years with multiple sclerosis, her weight, and, eventually, a brain tumor. She radiated delight when she saw you, made every new person that she met feel special, and every interaction with old friends seem like a special occasion. She was able to step into leadership roles because people she met trusted her integrity—her wholeness and her authenticity. Her whole being was present in every moment and she brought that energy to her leadership roles, so that she attracted others to her, but she never presumed to be better than anyone else. She had that light that made her a special person.

Very likely when you see someone like my friend, who sadly died of complications of the brain tumor, you are in the presence of a shaman. Light is, of course, energy. People of light like my friend seem to exude energy, positive energy, no matter what their other problems might be. And shamans work with energy. Somehow, as the popular saying goes, they "get over themselves" so that they are inherently able to recognize the worth and dignity of others, allowing others to recognize those qualities in themselves.

So, shamans can be found in virtually any walk of life or set of activities where the intention of the individual is to make the world a better place. Remember your favorite teacher, and think about the magic that she or he seemed to perform in the classroom—engaging deeply with both learners and the material, ensuring that everyone was on board with the learning agenda. She or he might not have even been a particularly "nice" person. I remember my high-school English teacher. She was the one everyone feared. But we learned! Oh, how we learned, and she delighted in our learning, was proud of us, and we knew it. Perhaps you know someone like that: a psychologist, social worker, the barista at the local coffee shop, the administrative assistant who always greets you happily and cheers your day, the carpenter or custodian who brings light into the room while servicing it, or someone in some other type of work who seems to be able to deeply engage with everyone he or she meets in ways that profoundly move them along the path to healing.

Me? Don't I have to be perfect?

The shaman's light clearly has any number of ways of shining. Perhaps that person of light is already you if let your light shine through. Or, if you can find your own source of joy, meaning, and connection within and are willing to give it to others, perhaps it can be you. Maybe my story will help.

Years ago, I began reading numerous books about shamans, including some by Western anthropologists, psychologists, and physicists who had ventured into the world of shamanism. With all this reading, I began to think about what it might mean to be or become a shaman in today's world. Would it involve mysterious rituals and rites, seeing or calling "souls" that others could not see, working with people whose spirits were somehow sick and becoming their healer? How, if at all, might being a shaman apply to the work that I did every day as a professor of management? How might being a shaman, in fact, apply at all in our modern world, where the term is hardly known and even less accepted, except in what most people view as "new age" or circles of people that many of my acquaintances and colleagues considered wacky at best?

For the most part, even in books that tried to modernize the concept, shamanism's ways seemed entrenched in traditional and Indigenous practices and cultural artifacts with all of these cultures' mythologies and beliefs about the natural world and spirits. Although these approaches are appealing in many ways, they seemed vastly different from everything familiar to the scientifically informed worldview of a culturally Western woman, steeped as I was in a business school environment, or, for that matter, most of my friends, similarly steeped in urbanized, Western cultures.

What, after all, is a shaman? Shaman: the very word calls up mysterious and unfamiliar images of Indigenous medicine men and women. Further, traditional shamans tend to focus their healing on individual patients and the surrounding community, while I was clearly not about to undertake that type of healing. So, before we go any further, I have a confession to make. I often felt and sometimes still feel like a complete fraud when it comes to being or becoming a shaman. It is, somehow, not for me to say that I am a shaman, but rather for others to recognize that my work has put me into the category of shaman, if indeed it has done so. Further, whatever gifts I might have, they do not seem to be the powers or gifts of communing with spirits or "seeing" them, or the psychic powers that other "real" (to my mind) shamans seem to have that help heal others.

For years, it seemed that I had to get to be shamanically (and humanly) "perfect" (whatever that means) in some way before I could talk or write about shamanism in any coherent kind of way, particularly in ways that might be acceptable professionally. Certainly, it seemed that I needed to have the same kinds of shamanic experiences that others appeared to have—seeing or hearing spirits, getting insights psychically, sensing things before they happen, empathically feeling what others are feeling, or being able to sense and use energy in powerful ways to help heal others or something in the world. Something that suggested out-of-the ordinary experiences. Combined with an innate skepticism about all things spiritual or intuitive, and despite a long-standing interest in and study of shamanism, I was entirely skeptical that any shamanic gifts were open to me.

Nonetheless, after years of hesitating and working around edges of thought and practice that I (and, I presumed, many of my academic colleagues) considered strange or weird, I ultimately entered into study of shamanic practice with, John Myerson. An African-tradition-trained shaman and, probably not incidentally, also PhD psychologist, Buddhist priest, yogi, high-order swordsman and martial artist, and acupuncturist, John translated his knowledge and insights into thinking about the power associated with the shaman without ritual, without particular traditions or belief systems, and through practices familiar these days to many Westerners, including meditation and visualization. John, who has now written three books on his shamanic experiences, [16] soon had me meditating and journeying, sensing in new ways, and over the course of a few years working with a group of other interested people in our "Way of Power" group, a group that is still ongoing as I write. There is a Buddhist proverb that says "when the student is ready, the teacher will appear." And that is what happened for me.

Over many years of working with meditations and journeys, of trying to sense various energies around me, as well as working with the "Way of Power" group that John started, I began to have some degree of trust in my own powers—though they are hardly traditional or accepted shamanic powers. Through the years, particularly from John's teaching without ritual or particular practices (which admittedly was frustrating to some of us in the group at times), it became clearer that shamanism today need not be embedded in traditional rituals, ceremonies, and practices. It also ("finally!", according to the Way of Power group members) began to dawn on me that shamanic gifts come in many flavors. At times, the Way of Power group did experience some more traditional ways of entering into shamanic journeys, i.e., through drumming sessions, meditations, or short rituals when we demanded them. Most of the time, though, we entered into the shamanic state either through a variety of meditative practices or by simply sitting quietly with the group—or elsewhere—and sensing what "came up."

Something similar to that—it finally became clear to me— happened with my work as well. My day job, if you will, is that of professor of management, and I have, over time, worked on issues relating to multi-sector collaboration, business in society, corporate responsibility, management education, and, more recently, large system change (among other topics) to deal with the issues of climate change, sustainability, and social justice. Numerous times over the course of my career, I have been at the edge of something new or some new ways of thinking about these things. It was only through the work with the Way of Power group and with John that I finally came to realize that not everyone has the "luck" or what the great psychologist Carl Jung called "synchronicity" to be in the right places to access new information.

Because my imagination is not populated with mythological figures, as the minds of many in Indigenous cultures are, or with spirits of various sorts, as the minds of people who are religious can be, and because I was not living in a context close to nature, I was not receiving information from guides, power animals, or angels. They simply were not in my imaginal vocabulary (see Chapter 4 for more background on the imaginal realm). But, as the group powerfully pointed out to me one day, my mind (imagination, psyche, spirit) was going "somewhere," very quickly and then returning, gathering information or insights when they were needed. I call that process "going to the imaginal realm." It is that capacity and willingness to call upon what psychologists refer to as the collective unconscious that I now believe is a deep source of shamanic power, insight, and healing energy. The capacity to go to that place deep within is a source of power that is available to everyone if they can quiet down enough to seek it and work to develop their own insight. This quieting often takes place through meditative and reflective practices (see "Practice: there is no one way" in Chapter 4), and can recognize the information when it comes.

My particular gift, such as it is, appears to be a capacity to connect across ideas, linking them sometimes in ways that not many others are yet doing, and crossing disciplinary boundaries, which enables new ways of thinking to emerge. Some of that capacity involves a willingness to trust my instincts—intuition—that something is right or that a certain way of thinking needs to evolve even when others are initially skeptical or downright negative about the idea. Some of it involves trusting what we in the group came to call "the universe" and I, following Jung, generally call the collective unconscious. Depending on your own tradition, you may wish to call it the One, Spirit, the Universe, God, or some other name. Indeed, some physicists (and many mystics) now believe that consciousness itself is the ground of existence and that we are all interconnected with each other, all other aspects of the universe,[17] and hence consciousness, which would make that consciousness accessible to us if we know how to access it—and are willing to do so.

Insight can happen very quickly when I need to "see" something, such as (in my case) when I am writing and ideas get connected in new ways. Sometimes new documents, issues, papers, emails, and people synchronistically present ideas that I need in a sort of just-in-time way, when I am "ready" to see them. Once I was essentially gifted with an entire book—whatever I needed to write and the inspiration for the shape of the book basically came through me and poured out of me without a lot of will on my part.

We are all products of our own cultural backgrounds and belief systems. That background and set of beliefs influences what we believe to be real and the mythologies that we call upon in shamanic states and for shamanic guidance. Depending on your own cultural background, imaginal experiences, and how you envision the source of your power, you may well find that you call upon power animals, spirit guides, religious figures, ancestors, other people, or other imaginal beings providing information and insight to you, much as most books on shamanism will tell you to do.

There are any number of good books on shamanism and shamanic techniques that can guide you towards more traditional methods, and some good ones that adapt those methods to modern times, though typically still drawing on power animals, spirit guides, and the like.[18] Since we are all products of our cultures, our imaginations provide sources that are culturally relevant to us—but may not be to others. My own *lack* of imagination in that respect means that I don't see such beings, but that says nothing about how you will experience your insights, since your background and imagination is different. We will explore this type of imaginal experience in more detail when we look more deeply at the connecting role of the shaman in Chapter 3.

That said, with my more or less scientifically trained mind and pretty rational Western sensibility, I remain skeptical about all things associated with shamanism . . . and try to figure out what works and what doesn't from some sort of testable hypothesis perspective. At the same time, I have learned to trust my own instincts when I am able to let universe flow through me and hope that my work has done some good in the world. So, eventually I realized that shamanic power is not about perfection or one specific way of engaging with the world. For me, and I hope for you, it is about finding and using whatever powers and capacities you have to the fullest to bring about positive change in the world. You don't need to be perfect to try to do that. You simply need to put your own energy out there with the intent of helping . . . and work to accept the gifts that you are given, whatever they might be.

Not being perfect means that we make mistakes sometimes. It means that not everything we do is as helpful or healing as we might wish it be. It can mean that we recognize ourselves as flawed human beings with good intentions—and it also means that we take the necessary risks and do the necessary work to put ourselves into the best possible position to be able to undertake whatever helping it is our purpose to do. It means we work through our own fears and try to heal ourselves spiritually (and psychically and emotionally) so that we are able to do the work in the world that we are called to do. I believe that everyone can be a shaman today if they are willing to put the work in and take the risks inherent in the shaman's role.

The questions for you are: What are *your* shamanic powers? How will you uncover them? And how will you use them?

3

Today's shaman's work: healing, connecting, sensemaking

This chapter explores the three main functions of the shaman—healing, connecting, and sensemaking—which are undertaken in the service of a better world. Shamans can be powerful figures in their relevant communities, so the orientation towards a better world—or healed patients and communities in the case of traditional shamans—is important. These three tasks are deeply interrelated, although they are conceptually teased apart below. The reality is that they are connected to each other and when, for example, a shaman is engaged in healing, there is also connecting and sensemaking going on, and so with the other main tasks.

Healing

The literal meaning of healing is "to make whole," or to bring about balance in an organism or system that has become unbalanced. The words "heal," "healer," "healing," "health," "wholeness," "holistic," and "holy" all derive from the same root word: the Old English "hal." Considering these related words together suggests that a key aspect of healing is to help bring about wholeness in a person, community, or system of some sort. Healing can also take place in a relationship (for example, the relationship between a person and another), with a community, in the context of an organization, or between the person and nature. Entire communities and organizations may need to be "made whole" through a healing process, which is what scholars Peter Frost and Carolyn Egri wrote about when they referred to organizational development specialists and change agents as shamans.[19]

The healing process is fundamentally a task of healing relationships of all sorts[20] and is the foremost task of the shaman, no matter what the culture or setting. Notably the idea of health, healing, and wholeness is aligned with another important word for the shaman: integrity, which also means wholeness or soundness, as well as honesty, freedom from corruption, and moral soundness. In this sense, today's shaman's work is that of change agent,[21] helping to change relationships for the better, whether those relationships are interpersonal, organizational, or systemic.

Today, the Earth itself is in trouble, or, more accurately, humankind's relationship with the Earth is problematic. A diseased (dis-eased) or disordered (dis-ordered) system is one that needs healing—to be brought back into ease and order, i.e., coherence. For example, today's economic system, which is oriented towards constant growth, combined with population growth, has pushed many ecosystems beyond their sustainable limits and led to human-induced climate change, according to the vast majority of climate scientists. Inequality, the gap between the rich and poor, has been growing, too, to levels that have already created discontent and disruption in many places around the world, particularly when combined with lack of decent livelihoods for far too many people.

When things in nature go out of order—out of the natural order of things—there are always dynamics that bring disordered ecosystems back into some semblance of order, sometimes harshly or in extreme circumstances through collapse to a simpler state. If one species, for example, takes over in an ecosystem and uses up too many resources, soon enough food supplies for that species are diminished. Pushed too far, the whole system collapses or that particular population collapses, ultimately resulting in a new order or sense of balance, but not one that might have been desirable.

Human population growth coupled with an economic system that pushes constant growth and material consumption is pretty much beyond dispute, pushing our ecosystems beyond limits that might keep the system in balance. This growth orientation of today's economy, combined with overuse of fossil fuels, population growth, and production practices that strip land, ocean, and air of their ability to sufficiently regenerate needed balance, has resulted in a context of climate change and sustainability problems, not to mention many moral conundrums. Too many ecosystems are moving towards collapse, and climate change, according to an overwhelming majority of climate scientists, could pose existential threats to great portions of the human population.

Indeed, scientists across disciplines have suggested that several of nine identified planetary boundaries have already been breached,[22] threatening humanity's very future. Growing gaps between the rich and the poor create even more problems. For example, we now see a level of inequality that could lead to an escalation of the worldwide social disruption already being witnessed. Add in issues with energy, food production and distribution, growing practices in agriculture and animal husbandry, terrorism, conflict among ethnic and religious groups, among many others, and there is no shortage of relationships on the planet that need healing—and where people who know how to work with their shamanic gifts can be useful.

Since the healing work of the shaman is to create order from what is dis-ordered and ease from what is dis-eased, it can be applied whether that system is a person, a community, an organization, or a whole system of some sort. Healing can occur through new relationships, insights, ideas, artistic expressions, or any number of other ways. In fact, many people that I consider to be shamanic are working today restoring order, harmony, and balance at the level of the world as a whole. Indeed, Serge Kahili King, author of *Urban Shaman*,[23] actually defines the shaman as a "healer of relationships." Those relationships might be within families or between spouses, between parents and children, among friends and relatives, or within a given community. Each of us has a role to play in healing the relationships that exist in the world—and not creating even more fractures than already exist: the opposite of being a shaman.

Finding purpose

Purpose is a reason for doing something. Finding your purpose can be an important part of the healing process for yourself. As with much shamanic experience, achieving and even finding purpose requires both intention and attention. Purpose provides a rationale for doing something and also an impetus for continuing to learn, do, and experience something because it is central to who we are as human beings. Purpose gives meaning to our lives; hence finding out what our particular purpose is, particularly as healer, connector, and sensemaker, is particularly important to the shaman.

A sense of purpose can, for example, make a difference in whether you are willing to recognize and "allow" the shamanic experiences that we all have to help you figure out your life's passions and paths, and ultimately to bring your gifts to the world. The call to shamanism is, like any calling, a strong desire or urge to move towards a particular purpose, way of life, or type of work. The nature of the shaman's work of healing, connecting, and sensemaking in the service of the greater good can certainly be associated with answering the call. There is a sense in which, once you recognize the nature of the shamanic experience, it is hard to turn back or away from it—and to the extent that you answer the call, you put yourself in service of some purpose bigger than yourself. That, simply put, is the nature of the shaman's work.

The idea of purpose gives meaning to our lives, however you define your particular purpose. As we have already seen, the calling to purpose of the shaman can be manifested in many different ways. There is no one "right" way, though a key is that you are serving something "beyond self," something that some might say is "bigger" than yourself and somehow contributes positively to the world. In other words, it would be hard to say that that an individual who simply wants to acquire more wealth or material goods for him- or herself was pursuing a shamanic purpose.

At the same time, if the shamanic call comes, then it is important to open up to the possibilities that being shaman present to you. Doing so can help you shape a meaningful life where you understand the ways in which what you do contributes to others and to the world around you. Answering the call to purpose was certainly important for the academics that I studied as "intellectual shamans." Many of them expressed that they did the work that they did because, in a very real way, they could not *not* do it. They were called to it, even if doing what they did meant some risk to their careers. For example, some focused on issues of sustainability in the early days of that concept's traction, even though they were warned that doing so would be a "career killer." Similarly for others, focusing on positive aspects of organizations, when most others focused on negative aspects, was the direction of their calling—despite skepticism from many traditional scholars about the worth of doing so.

Given the power of purpose in our lives, it is important to reflect on the question of what it is that you are called to do or be, through whatever reflective practices make the most sense to you. Who are you meant to be? With the intellectual shamans, I called this process "becoming fully who you are." That sense of authenticity—to yourself and *your* distinct calling or purpose—is the key, not what others might want you to do. In becoming fully who you are, you need to figure out at least the initial steps in moving in that direction, and then, in a sense "allow" what happens to open you to other possibilities along the way. We will explore more about answering your particular call to purpose and what it means to become fully who you are in Chapter 4.

Healer, heal thyself

Some believe that to become a shaman you have to go through great trauma and transitions. There is certainly a very real sense in which shamans have to heal themselves before they can begin to heal others, communities, mythologies, or the world around us. This process can be difficult. Sometimes it is necessary to go through a major transition in life—a sort of death and rebirth—that opens us up to new ways of knowing and being in the world. In that process, we can "allow" the experiences that are beyond ordinary reality to come into our consciousness. It is also true that many traditional shamans experienced life-transforming events, vision quests, decided differences from others, or life-threatening illnesses in their path to shamanism. Others, of course, learn shamanism in traditional societies through an apprenticeship, though that, too, frequently involves some hardship. Partly, coming to shamanism is being open to the learning and insight such experiences can provide and turning them to healing purposes rather than letting traumatic or difficult experiences make us bitter or negative.

By a certain age, most of us have been through numerous experiences and transitions that can, if experienced as opportunities for learning and enhancement, be part of the path to becoming the shaman. It all depends on how we deal with them. Rather than viewing such experiences merely as depressing or problematic, what if we can learn from them? For example, do we let them heal or hurt us? Do we wallow in trauma, negative memories and thoughts, or figure out some way, perhaps through reflection, reframing of the situation, distance and time, and a new perspective, to "rise above" the trauma, negative experiences, sadness, or challenges we face? Do we gain insight from mistakes, problems, and traumas, or simply cower before them, resting in the fear that is part of simply being alive? Do we let such experiences "get" to us and define us in some way, or do we find ways to let them go and move beyond them in the interests of something bigger than ourselves? In part, it is our response to life events that determines whether they knock us down or help uplift us, whether we can learn what we need to learn from them, so that we can take that learning and help others with it.

The shamanic question is: how can we find a way for even very traumatic events to change us for the better? Traumas like the death of a loved one, or a serious accident, for example, or much less traumatic but still difficult experiences like moving to a new city, taking on a new more challenging position—enlightening educational, artistic, or intense interpersonal engagements—can all act as a spur to shamanic insight. Depending on how we respond to such events, they can hurt us deeply, create depression, and paralyze us. Or they can be used as learning experiences that help us to find ways to love ourselves, move beyond the fear that is natural, and help others. If we take the latter approach, the learning and insight approach, then we are on the path to becoming a shaman.

Heal yourself first, and then . . .

Since we are all damaged in some way just because of living, damage can get in the way of healing others or the world, if we let it. For example, we can feel that we were not given enough love or attention from our parents, or that others have ignored us or treated us badly. Some people, of course, have actually been abused in various ways. Illnesses of all sorts can cause emotional, psychological, and spiritual damage, as well as physical problems. Failing to accomplish some desired goal or being cheated can damage us. Damage can occur in any number of ways simply because we are living in a complex world. Such emotional, psychological, and spiritual damage creates "baggage" that can make us angry, unresponsive, or self-indulgent, preventing us from taking healing actions towards ourselves, others, or the world around us. For that reason, self-healing is needed before the shaman can begin to work to heal others or the world around him or her.

Importantly, self-healing needed for the emotional, psychological, and spiritual wounds of life is not necessarily a once and done thing. It mostly can be conceived of as a process, sometimes a long-term process. From my own experience, it is a never-ending process; no one is ever completely healed. Not only have we all been damaged simply by the process of living, but new hurts are readily accumulated until and unless you can learn to simply "let them go": that is, not attach to them. Buddhists talk about this process of non-attachment as a way of giving up the suffering that is part of life, attained through mindfulness and meditation practices. So there is always some distance to go, some new thing that needs to be healed.

The reality of the need for ongoing healing means that it is important not to fall into the trap that you can't become shamanic or do healing work until you are fully healed, because most likely you will never be fully healed. If you wait until you are "perfect" in some way, chances are you will never embark on the healing work that you are meant to do. Rather, heal what you can in yourself—and then turn your energies towards healing others or whatever aspect of the world around you that you can influence.

The question, of course, is *how* to heal yourself, whether from physical injury, emotional or mental trauma, or life events, as you pursue a shamanic path. Sometimes, allopathic medicine or "alternative" approaches are needed to engage the physical healing process. Often, particularly for emotional, psychological, and spiritual healing, something more is needed. Sometimes psychological therapy can help, particularly for emotional and mental traumas and issues. The shamanic approach to healing takes place, in addition to these "ordinary" (Western) approaches, in a spiritual context as well, for in some very real way it is our spirit—our energy—that must be healed.

Shamanic healing typically involves the spiritual aspects of what needs to heal. Such healing can encompass forgiveness of yourself and others for injuries they have done to you. It can mean developing compassion for yourself first, then for others, then for the world more generally, and for nature. It can mean sending love and healing energy through the power of your imagination to yourself in the condition in which you were injured or hurt and seeing yourself healed: for example, getting the love that you felt was lacking, or responding to an insult with love and forgiveness instead of rage and pain. It can mean allowing a sadness or sense of loss that you feel to fully surface, facing it and accepting that it exists, without allowing it to overpower and overwhelm you. Healing can mean sending love and positive energy to that place in you that experiences the sadness, loss, or hurt and allowing it to heal in the context of what can be experienced shamanically—in non-ordinary states of consciousness or trance states—as a vast source of love that comes from wherever you believe such love exists, e.g., from your own inner resources, from the universe, or from some higher power.

Often healing can mean "walking through some sort of fear," since fear or being threatened in some way can be at the core of an injury or hurt that needs to be healed. By walking through the fear I mean doing something like envisioning the cause of your hurt and powerfully facing it. It could mean simply envisioning imaginally what it would be like to go past that fear in some way, to *be* in the world without that hurt hanging over you. Particularly for issues associated with fear, getting assistance from either an experienced shamanic teacher, healer or other professional to help you move through this experience can be really helpful. It can be difficult to learn to face fear, sadness, anger, hurt, rejection, and similar emotions on your own. We will talk more about fear in Chapter 5, because it is a powerful force that can prevent us from being fully who we need to be if we let it, just as staying in a state of fear can prevent us from doing the healing work so necessary in the world today, keeping us in a state of being threatened, angry, resentful, and strident.

That inner light that shamans, or people with what I earlier called strange attractors, seem to have reflects their energy. Perhaps it reflects the extent to which healing has taken place and the person has become whole. The light, the energy, the healing could come from a sense of peace that they have attained through the necessary process of healing themselves before they can attempt to heal others. I remember how much calmer I seemed internally once I was able to accomplish what my teacher called "connecting" with source or the universe—or myself and the collective unconscious. Having been brought up Catholic, though long since "recovering," I suppose that such a direct "connection" to the universe or to whatever we mean by something beyond the self was not encouraged. Thus, when my teacher directed me to meditate on love (a form of Buddhist meditation) and I was able to directly sense that love, something shifted in me and it felt like an internal source of light.

Shamanic healing, which engages with spirit, can enhance other forms of treatment because it provides a more holistic approach. For example, one shamanic approach that is frequently used in the group I work with is: when there is a problem, go deep within yourself (often in a meditative or trance state) and ask, "what part of you needs to be healed?" Sometimes it is an older self, perhaps you as a child or adolescent, perhaps it is an ancestor, perhaps it is a current part of yourself that emerges as needing healing. One process for providing the needed healing, absent a teacher or shaman to help, is to envision that part of you being fully loved, healed, and accepted by the "you" who exists today. Then you can let go of whatever old trauma is creating today's trauma. Such processes of healing can take time and repetition, especially if you are trying to heal on your own, and can be aided by a caring teacher who helps you gain insight into what it is that you need to heal, in a spiritual sense, before moving on. Of help here are many of the shamanic techniques of journeying discussed briefly in Chapter 5 and in many popular books on shamanism that are technique-oriented.

One of the things that my teacher always says when discussing a wound, particularly a spiritual, psychological, or emotional one, is to "send love" to the part of you that is wounded. "Sending love" is probably insufficient to resolve all ills, but, without recognizing the importance of loving wounded parts of yourself, you are likely to remain "stuck" in the mire of emotional, psychological, and sometimes intellectual baggage. Through such approaches you can find meaning in what has caused the wound, relate that wound somehow to a bigger picture and a bigger sense of who you are and who you serve in the world. Healing in the shamanic sense, then, means going beyond the self while simultaneously caring for the part of you that is wounded. It means finding the bigger purposes and reasons why wounds have taken place, and then finding a place where you can both love and let go of those wounds. It means forgiving what needs to be forgiven, and, in a sense, "allowing" (see Chapter 5) a new perspective, based in love, to take the place of the old one.

Based on what we have just discussed, clearly shamanic healing has a spiritual element to it. It is about shaping new meanings out of old ones, creating new stories where the old ones no longer work—both for self and for others—and making new linkages that help reframe experience in new and more constructive ways. These connecting and sensemaking functions, then, as we'll discuss next, are vital elements of the shamanic perspective. Shamanic healing goes beyond physical, psychological, and emotional healing and provides for a more holistic approach that involves your own spirit—and possibly "Spirit" in the broadest sense. From that perspective, shamanic healing can potentially supplement the other approaches typically used in Western culture, such as psychological therapy, allopathic medicine, and other types of supportive approaches to emotional and psychological wounds. Such techniques may not always be enough in and of themselves, but healing the internal hurts that we have inevitably experienced in life's course can be an important part of the overall healing journey.

Integrity and holistic thinking

Because of their healing function, today's shamans, like traditional shamans, as healers, also need personal integrity—wholeness—to do their healing work of enhancing soundness and wholeness in what needs repair. The word "integrity" means a sort of uprightness of spirit, honesty, and constructive orientation. Integrity and wholeness—healing—also connote the sacred nature of the work of the shaman through another word with similar roots to healing: holy. The idea that shamanic work is holy links the shaman's healing to the sometimes spiritual meaning-making, integrity-producing, and wholeness-making task of the shaman,. This idea is also reflected in the holistic (or systemic) thinking that is typical of the shaman. All of these interrelationships suggest that the work of the shaman always needs to be approached with integrity and with a concern for others and the world around us, not solely for our own wellbeing.

There is another reason that shamans always need to act with integrity: shamans have power. Because they have power, shamans need to adhere to a kind of shamanistic code of conduct that asks them to work for the highest good of the person, community, institution, or system that they are healing. If they are working at the individual level, shamans should always do that work with the person's permission. If working as part of a community that itself has integrity and recognizes a set of moral or artistic values to which community members adhere, the shaman needs to adhere to that community's moral or artistic standards, working toward the higher good of all.

The very word "integrity" carries meanings of honesty and fairness as well as completeness or wholeness. Because of the power inherent in the shaman's ability to bring about change—being a change agent through healing, connecting, and sense-making functions—shamans always need to work with care and integrity.

Shamans have power, because of who they are and how they act in their communities. They have power because they tap deep sources of knowledge and potential wisdom, and because they have allowed their instincts and insights to be honed and sharpened. But not all individuals consider the best interests of the community and others around them. Some would use their power for reasons that cannot be construed as healing. When shamans use their power for personal gain, to hurt others, or in other ways that cause harm, they are called sorcerers.

Since we are interested here in the positive use of shamanic power, we are focused not on sorcerers, but on shamans in their healing capacity. But it is important to recognize that shamanic power to heal relationships can be misused, highlighting the importance of always keeping integrity in mind in our actions as shamans, and working to disempower any shamanic individuals who tend towards misuse of that power. If you want to think about how sorcerers could misuse power, think of some of the charismatic people you have known or seen in the media—and how some of them abuse people and generally use their charms for self-interested purposes.

Today's shamans think, as shamans have always done, integrally (with integrity) or holistically. But that type of thinking can be difficult when so much of our world is fractured into disciplines, organizations, institutions, sectors, political, religious, and ethnic divides, and narrowly framed ideas and theories. Somehow we in the Western world have come to think that we can understand things, even living beings, through atomization: that is, by breaking them down into their smallest components and then hoping that somehow the big picture of the whole can be put together.

Some would say this separation of things into the smallest element—or atomization and fragmentation—comes about in part because of the 17th-century French philosopher René Descartes' idea that "I think, therefore I am," which separated mind and body, and has greatly influenced Western culture. This approach to understanding wholes can be compared to the children's verse about Humpty Dumpty—the egg once broken can never really be put back together again.

Still, physics now tells us that everything is connected at the quantum level. From that reality, we can get a sense that perhaps traditional shamans were correct when they put forward the idea that you cannot separate mind and body or, for that matter, humans and nature. The emotional, psychological, spiritual, and imaginative influence each other, our physical beings, and general wellbeing holistically, in ways that are still not well understood by science. A traditional shaman has an implicit systemic understanding of this aspect of the world. When attempting to heal a patient, the shaman knows that the patient and the illness need to be considered in the context of the broader community. When working on communities, the shaman understands that relationships in the community may need to heal, and when working in bigger contexts the shaman tries to be aware of the systemic nature of the context and its dynamic influences, patterns, and relationships.

And so today's shaman understands that which needs to be healed in its broader context, be that a personal/individual, family, community, or world context. The shaman today knows that things cannot simply be separated from each other or fragmented into parts, but need to also be considered integrally, as a whole, if we hope to gain the healing that is needed in our fractured world. For example, today's business shaman understands business in the broader social, political, and ecological contexts—or ecosystems—as well as in the industry or competitive environment of the business. The shamanic teacher knows that the student exists in a family and community environment as well as a learning context within the school—and that these other environments influence the student's readiness and ability to learn. Dealing with the whole system in some way is important in helping the student learn or the business thrive, as examples. Similarly, the holistic perspective of the shaman enhances the capacity of people in other lines of work.

Thus, the shaman tends to look at the whole as well as the parts, because the whole is more than the sum of its parts; and simply taking apart a system and looking at the parts cannot tell the whole picture that is needed for healing purposes. The idea that we need to consider the whole not just the parts is particularly important when we think about living beings or systems. Because they are organic, it is easier to recognize the interconnectedness, interdependence, and interrelatedness of the parts of living systems than it is for non-obviously living systems, although non-living things also have a certain integrity. Certainly, living systems have a holistic integrity that needs to be recognized.[24]

For example, we cannot fully understand a human being, with all of our emotions, psychological elements, fears, hopes, and dreams by simply looking at blood or brain cells, nerves, and other physical components. Indeed, perhaps we can *never* fully understand a human being—or any other living creature or system. Nor can we understand humans simply by looking at economic theory's notion of *homo economicus*, which argues that humans always act in self-interested ways. Biology tells us differently, for humans and many other creatures sometimes act symbiotically and for the good of the community, not just their own good. While things like emotions, psychological issues, pain, love, or fears have physical manifestations that result in nerves firing or other physiological expressions, to really understand them we need to actually experience them—and that experience is not objective, but rather subjective.

The philosopher Ken Wilber[25] has noted, in developing what he calls an integral perspective, that to really understand something fully, i.e., wholly, we need to look at four aspects. Note here the link to integrity and holistic thinking discussed above. Wilber's integral framework argues living systems have four quadrants: two that are empirically observable, i.e., individual and group "objective" levels, and two that are subjectively experienced, i.e., interior or subjective individual aspects (e.g., psychological, emotional, spiritual) and group or collective experiences (e.g., cultural experiences, national identities, and the like). The subjective or "interior" aspects of living systems can only be understood, as Wilber points out, by asking the individual or participants what they are experiencing and finding ways to validate that they are telling the truth.

From Wilber's perspective, the internal experiences of conscious beings, like us humans, play an important role in how we experience ourselves and others. Wilber's point is that any one perspective, while potentially valuable, does not provide sufficient information or insight into the whole system, organism, or person. He argues that understanding all four perspectives or quadrants is needed if we are to begin to fully understand what is going on—and heal the relationships that exist among elements within a given system. These ideas will be explored more deeply in Chapter 6.

One relationship that clearly needs healing today is the one between humans and nature, as noted above. The healing of this relationship is particularly in Western civilizations, where there has long been thought to be a separation between man [sic] and nature, where humankind has tended to believe it should have "dominion" over nature. Dominion has meanings of supremacy, dominance, mastery, authority, and control. This belief is distinctly different from the beliefs of many Indigenous shamans who understand that humankind is part of and deeply interconnected with all aspects of nature.

Further, believing that humans should reign supreme over nature takes away the understanding that now comes from physics, evolutionary biology, and the traditional wisdom of the shaman. This wisdom tells us that we humans are in fact deeply and inextricably interconnected and interdependent with nature. As we will explore later on, quantum physics now demonstrates that everything is fundamentally connected. We humans are unescapably *part* of nature, not separate from it or superior to it. Further, increasing our understanding of nature as what complexity scientists call a complex adaptive system, which is inherently complex and multifaceted with unpredictability built into it, suggests the futility of actually trying to "control" nature. Shamans know and understand these realities and work to understand the deep linkages and interdependencies that humankind has with nature.

An important shamanic insight that comes from being a healer focused on restoring harmony and balance to the whole of some system is understanding the need to restore an appropriate balance between humans and nature. This balance recognizes that we cannot exist without nature and that the health of the natural environment is absolutely essential in supporting a thriving world that supports human needs and interests. Nature is not, in fact, there for humans to "exploit" as much as possible for personal (company or organizational) gain. Nature has provided a context in which human beings and their civilizations could evolve in mutually supportive, interactive ways, with nature providing necessary resources and dynamic conditions for human flourishing to occur.

When the crucial balance is shifted in favor of exploitation of natural resources beyond what the Earth can readily restore, things go out of balance, and there is the risk that Earth will no longer supply sufficient or the right kind of resources to support human civilizations. It is that risk, indeed, that today's climate change and sustainability crises pose for humanity—and it is an existential risk that increasingly calls for the healing powers and orientation of the shaman in all of us.

The split in Western cultures between mind and body—and similarly between spirit and science—is longstanding, but advances in quantum physics, complexity science, chaos theory, and the idea of self-organizing systems tell us that this conceptual split does not work. Shamans recognize this emerging understanding of reality and act in more integrated ways as part of their healing processes. Shamans today need to understand that science and spirituality are different ways of knowing: both are important and not necessarily contradictory, simply different (i.e., first person vs. third person); this is something that Wilber also argues for.[26]

Having an integral or holistic perspective of living systems, which combines all four of the individual subjective and objective and the collective subjective and objective perspectives, as Wilber has argued, can help advance understanding—and healing in the world. Such an integral perspective is intended to improve the world, make it more whole, more integrated overall. Shamans in their healing capacities care deeply about this wholeness and work towards it collaboratively, and in co-evolutionary ways, along with many others with the same agenda.

Connecting

The second major task in the work of the shaman is what I call "connecting." Scholars Peter Frost and Carolyn Egri described the connecting function as boundary-spanning or "mediating realities." The term "mediation" is interesting in this context because it implies that today's shaman is bridging, integrating, and reconciling the differences that might exist in many aspects of life. This bridging occurs, for example, between two realms, two or more people, within a group or organization, or among different ideas, mythologies, ideologies, and belief systems, as examples. The bridging might take place between ordinary reality and some sort of narrative, story, or artistic view of that reality as evidenced in, for example, a painting, drawing, photograph, poem, or story.

Connecting allows for linking ideas, insights, media, systems, disciplines, theories, people, and other things that perhaps are not generally put together. For traditional shamans, this mediation of boundaries takes place between our ordinary world and the world of spirit, usually in the trance or altered state of consciousness. Shamans generally believe that everything, including inanimate objects, has spirit. Spirit from this perspective is in other people, in animals and other living beings, and also in manifestations of nature that we typically do not consider to be "alive."

Through the connecting function, shamans build on this sense of spirit in all, which we will discuss in terms of dignity for all of nature's manifestations in Chapters 5 and 7. Connecting means making linkages, perhaps linkages that others do not readily see, across boundaries where others perhaps choose not to venture. Traditional shamans venture in what are called "journeys" to spiritual realms, where they pick up information not readily accessible in our ordinary world. I believe that in doing so, they (and we) are tapping into the collective uncon- scious, or perhaps deep inner wisdom that we all have if we are open to it. That wisdom comes from the universe (call it the One, Spirit, God[s], angels, or whatever you like) and can be available to us if we move into what is called a shamanic state of mind, i.e., a trance or hypnotic state, sometimes called an altered state of mind.

The shamanic state of consciousness in which journeying takes place can be induced in any number of ways. In traditional cultures, drugs that cause hallucinations or dreamlike states are sometimes used. Other cultures use drumming, chanting, sing- ing, gongs, bells, or other repetitive rhythmic means of inducing the trance state. Trance can also be achieved through meditative and mindfulness practices, and through various physical activi- ties. If you have ever experienced a "runner's high," or driven somewhere and can't remember how you got there, you have experienced a trance state. Activities like qi gong, yoga, and some martial arts can induce this state, as can just about any repetitive exercise or activity.

Some people experience this shamanic state of consciousness in relationships when they are deeply engaged with another per- son intellectually, emotionally, or physically. Some people expe- rience it in work or artistic activities like painting, drawing, playing music, sewing, or doing any hobby that challenges and engages them fully. Sometimes whole teams experience this state when everything seems to be clicking. During such states, peo- ple lose track of time and in a way "become" the activity in which they are engaged: that is, when there is no apparent sepa- ration between the person doing the activity and the activity itself. Psychologist Mihály Csíkszentmihályi calls this experience the state of "flow."[27]

In the trance or flow state we, in a sense, let down our rationalistic and analytical guard. It is in that state that we can "allow" insights to arise that might be there otherwise but are masked by rationality, thought processes that prevent us from seeing them, or the narratives and stories we tell ourselves about what is "real" and what is not real. It is this ability to "allow" what is to *be* that provides acceptance of what is, and opens a space in your heart and soul for compassion, forgiveness, and love to emerge, especially around the hurts and injuries life may have handed you.

Not every trance state, however, leads to shamanic experiences or insights. For the altered state of consciousness to become shamanic, you need to open to the experience and insights that come from the experience. You also need to open up to the ways in which what is being experienced can be used for healing, connecting, or sensemaking purposes that enhance either the health of a person, organization, or some other aspect of the world. In other words, the shamanic state of consciousness has a certain intentionality around it that fosters a deliberate seeking of new information and linkages, new insights, and new healed relationships in the service of making the world somehow better.

For intellectual shamans, connecting means venturing across disciplinary and subject boundaries, working between theoretical ideas and the world of practice, integrating research ideas into teaching in novel ways, and otherwise making sense of things holistically, across multiple different perspectives. Connecting can mean linking ideas that others have not yet linked. It can mean quite literally "connecting" to another person, somehow recognizing, say, a kindred spirit, a person you wish to know, an old friend with whom the conversation never seems to let up and can always be picked up where it was left off. Or it can mean connecting different people who would benefit from knowing each other, linking ideas and ideologies in new ways, and creating new ways that perspectives can be shaped.

Connecting is the part of the shamanic process where new insights that can be used for healing purposes emerge. Today's shamans reach, bridge, or mediate across boundaries in whatever line of work they are engaged. Connecting means allowing the insight that arises from the collective unconscious, the creative impulse, the relationships among people, or the need that is present to become manifest. It means activating your instincts and seeing what makes sense when you take away the screen of rationality and analysis—which does not mean that analysis or rational/logical thinking is not important, but simply that it is insufficient.

Connecting and relationships

As we have noted, one definition of the shaman from Serge Kahili King is as a "healer of relationships."[28] Healing can take place in any number of relational contexts. Healing yourself by connecting with something deep in yourself, in the world, or with the universe (or spirit) is certainly one aspect of shamanism. Shamanism also focuses on the shaman's connection with others, and helping others connect with others. A further and vitally important aspect of shamanism is connecting with the world around us—nature and all of nature's creatures, as well s aspects of the world that we might not consider "living" in the normal realm of our activities. Healing relationships is fundamentally about connecting in constructive and restorative ways.

The idea of "connecting" with other people is common in our colloquial sense. We have all met someone with whom we immediately felt a bond—a connection—for whatever reason. That is a shamanic connection, based on some intuitive or perhaps energetic linkage that we recognize without being able to fully analyze. Connected relationships can be among people, of course, but they can also be with respect to humanity's relationship to the Earth, to the natural environment. Or they might be about the relationships of some of our organizations and institutions to each other or to their stakeholders. They could be about the relationships that integrally exist among all living species, or between obviously living creatures and the rest of nature. Connecting can be broadly defined as making such linkages—and also helping others to make them as well.

Connecting means making new "connections," e.g., among ideas and insights. In our ordinary "non-ordinary" frame of reference, this type of connecting is sometimes called the "aha!" moment: that moment of insight or intuition that pushes our creative or healing edge. For example, a shaman might make linkages among ideas, practices, disciplines, or relationships and people that others do not typically make or have not yet made. Traditional shamans connect in spiritual realms, gathering information for healing purposes, typically while the shaman is in a state of trance, which can be achieved in a variety of ways, including dance, drumming, chanting, meditation, and even drugs.

The connecting function is at its core an integration function, helping the shaman—and others through the sensemaking role—see things more holistically. Connecting inherently means crossing boundaries and, for the traditional shaman, those boundaries are generally into spiritual realms. Connecting involves recognition of interdependencies, interconnectedness, and interrelationships. Relationships with and among people are vitally important in building and enhancing communities, particularly when people are quite different from each other. Differences among peoples can occur in all sort of domains—values, beliefs, ethnic and religious backgrounds, cultural traditions, or, perhaps most simply, appearance and ability, to name just a few.

The art of connecting in small ways

One of the gifts of the shaman is to be able to recognize "the other," other people, as having inherent worth, or what Harvard scholar Donna Hicks calls dignity.[29] That recognition can be healing because it puts the shamanic person in a "fully present" state of mind that honors and values those people who are with him or her. Just being in the presence of someone who makes that kind of connection, who really "sees" or "gets" you can be a healing experience.

Such shamanic connecting need not be elaborate. We all know people who are shamanic and connect more easily than other people do. When these connections are with or between people, there are any number of ways that individuals can act in a healing, connecting, and/or sensemaking capacity. Many of these ways may not be immediately obviously shamanic. For example, if we think of the healing that comes from connecting very broadly, we can begin to get a sense of the wide range of ways that people may be interacting with us shamanically even when they don't recognize it. One of these ways is through connecting interpersonally in small (and sometimes bigger) ways—ways that have a healing impact.

Consider for a moment, those people that you interact with every day. Are there some people who make you feel special? Who are really *present* to you, fully there, and fully engaged with you? They may seem to give you a little gift of their full or authentic presence—making you feel recognized and "seen" in ways that other people simply don't. Interactions with them make you feel better because you know they, in a sense, witness part of you that more superficial interactions do not allow, and there is a certain grace in that witnessing. Such people can be found in all sorts of jobs and positions, not just in overtly healing capacities. For such people the capacity to present, fully here right now, fully engaged in whatever is going on, may be their particular shamanic gift.

Shamans in unexpected places and roles can be the people who make us smile. They provide that little bit of healing grace when they greet us. Consider the barista at your local coffee shop, who recognizes you and greets you happily in the morning, maybe even remembering what you typically order. It could be the receptionist at work, who does much the same thing, or perhaps the custodian, who views her or his work of cleaning as important to the wellbeing of those around them. Or the boss, friend, or family member who truly values what you do and sees you for who you really are. It could be a good friend who is willing to sit with you when you are sad, angry, or otherwise at your worst—and who still loves you, despite that worst.

University of Michigan scholar Jane Dutton, who has studied compassion and caring in organizations, talks about hospital workers—not the emergency-room staff or the nurses and doctors or technicians but the people who clean the rooms—as sometimes having this type of healing orientation in their work. The shamanic (my term, not Dutton's) individuals among these workers bring compassion to their jobs and really "see" the patients as people. They interact with patients and their families as individuals with feelings, personalities, and human needs in a setting that can be dehumanizing for many. And the interaction works best when it is reciprocated, so that patient, family, and worker feel seen and heard.[30]

I believe that individuals who are able to make these connections are undertaking the connecting role of the shaman, by creating linkages and relationships. Other connecting activities in the modern sense, of course, mean crossing sector, disciplinary, or other types of boundaries that create separate "worlds" or going to imaginal realms where new things can be experienced and brought back. Such activities are particular useful for artists and creative people, though anyone can use them. Shamans acting in the ways discussed here are also creating linkages that might not otherwise exist: healing, healthy, and whole relationships among people. Shamans acting in small ways make authentic connections, looking into our eyes and smiling, so that we feel just that much better than we did before we saw them. That is, we feel somehow healed. In making these connections, they can help us make sense of our day in new ways. Sometimes they just make the day a little better than it might otherwise have been simply in the way that they interact.

Here is an example of how apparently simple interactions can be healing. Many mornings on my way to work, I drive a route that takes me past a crossing guard, someone who helps children safely across the street as they go to school. A simple enough job, to be sure. But each time I go past him—an older gentleman, probably retired and doing this work as part of his retirement—he looks directly into my eyes and grins a genuine smile at me. Almost without exception, I feel better for that small bit of connection. I often wonder how many other people's days are made brighter because they interact with him in the same way. I'm sure that he doesn't consider himself a shaman in any respect. Indeed, he may never have heard the word, but he plays a definite healing role in my life when he makes that connection.

What if we all behaved that way towards others? That might be enough to begin to develop our own shamanic gifts and help us play a healing role towards others because we have learned how to connect in simple ways.

Connecting and seeing

When shamans journey in a trance or an altered state of consciousness, they are accessing what are called the "imaginal" realms, a term invented by Henri Corbin, who was an interpreter of Arabic and Persian texts.[31] Imaginal realms are realistic-feeling and -seeming imaginings that allow us to experience something "as if" it were happening in our everyday reality. The word "imaginal" comes from the Latin *imago*, which means image of god. Imaginal experiences fall somewhere between ordinary reality and strictly imaginary experiences, which we know to be imaginary, since imaginal experiences can feel and seem to be quite realistic. Corbin meant the term *imaginal* to apply to the soul or spirit, rather than the physical world of everyday.

Depending on your particular context, and the mythologies and belief systems that you adhere to, such imaginal realms might provide insights via, say, the types of power animals and spirit guides that traditional shamanic approaches suggest are important, angels and spirits, deities from your cultural background, or any other figures that can convey important information to you. It is from imaginal experiences that traditional and some of today's shamans derive the spirits and guides that help them to achieve insights, healing powers, the ability to connect, and, ultimately, to make sense of what they have learned. I'll discuss this in the section on sensemakers, because an important part of the work of the shaman as sensemaker is constructing new cultural mythologies—stories and narratives—to replace damaged old ones.

When we attempt to figure out where insights, bursts of creativity, and new connections come from, it is often from these imaginal realms, which shamans learn how to "visit." Visiting imaginal realms is achieved by either going into an altered state of consciousness or learning to "tune out" the noise of everyday existence and tune in to what needs to emerge. In this sense, connecting is closely linked to a skill that many shamans have—the ability to "see." This sense of being a seer of what is real means seeing, understanding, or knowing what needs healing, and how to go about starting the healing process, recognizing that people and systems in some way need to heal themselves.

Shamans, as is clear from the previous section, need to be able to "see" reality reasonably realistically and make connections that others are not making to be able to do their healing work. The word "seeing" is often used and the imaginal realm seems to imply some sort of visual experience of seeing things differently. Some people get their shamanic insights through other sensory functions—through hearing, feelings, gut senses or "knowings," tactile sensations, hunches, inspirations, intuition, sensing vibrations, smelling, or even tasting. "Seeing" as used here is actually a metaphor for however you experience those insights using the senses that dominate for you. For shorthand, we can call all approaches "seeing," since they each involve something appearing that seemed not to be present before the insight or connection was made.

Such seeing is linked to an aesthetic appreciation of the insight, in the sense of "that's beautiful." When a knowing, insight, or intuition comes, you are "connected" to the universe and whatever powers might exist in a different way than happens in everyday reality. Getting to that imaginal place can allow you to let go of enough of daily life to be open to different insights than would otherwise be available. The seeing that comes with connecting can demand courage, for seers are often ahead of their times, making connections that others have not yet made—and may not yet be ready to make. "Seeing" forces you to come to grips with sometimes uncomfortable aspects of reality or insights. Traditional shamans are actually trained to be able to cope with these imaginal experiences, and use their own cultural heritages to help them explain what they have seen in their sensemaking capacity, which will be discussed next.

Sensemaking

Many people consider the search for meaning to be the essence of spirituality in the non-denominational sense. The sensemaking function of the shaman is fundamentally about that meaning-making process. Sensemaking is the process of storytelling or constructing narratives, telling the truth as the shaman sees it, and helping others to see that truth. The shaman gains healing insights, which can be symbols, words, images, stories, songs, visions, phrases, linkages of ideas, and more, through experiences of non-ordinary states. Figuring out how to interpret and apply these insights is what is meant by the sensemaking process. Seeing on its own is not very helpful if we cannot make meaning out of what has been seen or if others, who need to, do not understand it. In a very real way, sensemaking is about developing narratives and storytelling. Those stories work best when they are culturally relevant and built on memes, or core cultural ideas, images, phrases, and symbols, that are resonant and widely shared.

The term "sensemaking" was popularized in organizational theory by Karl Weick, an extraordinary intellectual shaman and scholar, now retired from the University of Michigan.[32] Importantly, Weick noted that the sensemaking process means looking back on something—an experience or insight in the case of the shaman—and then interpreting it in some way, finding or constructing meaning out of it. One important aspect of sensemaking is that the shaman and his patient or community should be able to think, perceive, or act differently as a result of a powerful insight. Since shamanic insights can come in many forms, there are many possible interpretations of most insights, so the interprctive or sensemaking function is crucial in having the patient, community, organization, or other set of constituents understand and act on the insight.

The sensemaking role can in some respects be likened to that of seer or prophet. Prophets "call" reality as they see it and as it has been shown in non-ordinary reality. In that sense, sensemaking, while based on retrospective accounts of what has been seen, is future-oriented in that it represents an effort to (re-)shape the future. As will be discussed later, this approach to what shamans call shapeshifting can, in today's terms, be a form of change-making called shaping the shift.

As understood by Barbara Derwin, "Sense making assumes that the entire human package—body, mind, heart, soul—is simultaneously verbed, constantly evolving and becoming, and intricately intertwined."[33] Shamans, that is, are and act very much in this world as well as in whatever other worlds they operate in and can gather information from. In cultivating their imaginal capacity, shamans not only see what others may not yet see, they also need to develop the capacity to make sense out of what has been seen. Their core task, in some ways, is helping to heal "broken" cultural mythologies that are negatively influencing individuals (making them sick or dis-eased), organizations, institutions, and communities.

Cultural myths serve many functions in communities and societies. They can provide a sense of how individuals and the community relate to the broader world. They can tell us how we can and should relate to other people. They tell us who our "gods" and significant mythical (and real) figures are. They create archetypal images, symbols, and representations that give us our sense of identity and belonging in a given context or culture when we can relate to them. The importance of myths and the sensemaking function is perhaps one of the reasons that shamans are thought to have been among humanity's first storytellers, scientists, poets, and artists, among many other functions. Myths—stories and narratives—shape our beliefs, attitudes, and functioning in important ways. Myths in turn are shaped by the memes or core cultural artifacts that resonate broadly and combine in a variety of ways to make up these stories and narratives.

Stories we tell ourselves

The often spiritual and sometimes emotional and psychological "hurts" that shamans attempt to heal can be found in many respects in the stories that we tell ourselves. We can get caught up in negative stories about how our parents did not give us everything we needed, or what they did or did not do to and for us, and how therefore we are damaged for life. We can hold onto stories of hurts inflicted by others, whether family or friends, or by bosses or organizations, telling ourselves that we are helpless in the face of these hurts.

No one of any age in virtually any culture has grown up without some degree of damage, as discussed earlier. That damage persists to the extent that we tell ourselves that "this" and not "that" is our story. These stories that we tell ourselves open up possibilities for new ways of being in the world. Or they hold us back from attempting those new beliefs, behaviors, and actions because they reinforce our negative beliefs about ourselves or the world, about what we can and can't do in the world. Shamans know that if you change the story, you can change the beliefs, and ultimately change the behaviors that result from those beliefs.

If I constantly tell myself, for example, that no one loves me, chances are I will find fault in potential lovers and believe myself unworthy of love. Love is not likely to come my way. If I believe that I cannot learn the new skills needed in my job, then I am unlikely to put forth the effort necessary for learning those skills. Then, when I fail at the job, I will think even worse of myself. If I think that I am always unlucky, then it is likely that luck (which may be viewed as a combination of preparation, hard work, and recognition of opportunity) will come my way. My behaviors, in short, will reflect whatever stories I am telling myself.

The opposite is also true. If my story is that I can accomplish the task before me, then I will put forth the necessary effort. If I believe that love is available to me, I will move in the world with enough self-love that I become an attractor for others. Love is much more likely to come my way. Such is the power of sensemaking: how we make sense of the world is a direct reflection of the stories we tell ourselves—or that others have told us and we believed—about how the world is and how we are in the world. If we want to change, then we need to change the stories and associated beliefs.

As shamans in their sensemaking capacities do, we can construct new stories that help us to heal from the hurts life has thrown our way, negative beliefs, and stories that constrain us from achieving our full potential. Saying that we can construct a new story about who we are and how we are in the world does not mean that doing so is necessarily easy—but it can be done. Particularly if you can move yourself into a trance state, e.g., through meditative or mindfulness practices, reflective techniques, journaling, and related techniques, you can allow your subconscious thoughts and ultimately actions to shift.

Think about your "self-talk." What do you say when you make a mistake? Do you call yourself names and put yourself down, thinking that the mistake reflects your whole being in some way? Can you change that to be more positive? What if you viewed that mistake as an opportunity for learning how to do right what went wrong rather than dwelling on the negative? Years ago, a friend told me "Happiness is a choice." I have come to believe that he was correct, that it is about how we accept and perceive the inevitable trials and tribulations of life that ultimately determine our happiness, and what we do about them, that affects our state of mind. Personally, although I am not a huge meditator, I have found that meditative approaches to dealing with problems and issues can be very helpful in reframing what needs to be changed in my attitudes and beliefs.

During the trance that accompanies meditation and many reflective and mindfulness practices, we can be open, in a sense, to positive suggestions and new "stories" that we can give ourselves.

Think about what happens when you meditate, reflect, talk with your friends, or write in your journal. Can you find hope and positivity, a new positive story, rather than laying blame for your problems on others? What can you do to find love in yourself *for* yourself and all the hardships that you have faced? Meditation, yoga, mindfulness practices of all sorts, affirmations, and visioning processes, among other approaches, can be helpful as you try to shift your own story, make sense of a new one—and heal yourself, which we have already seen is important in becoming a shaman. Good coaches, like shamans, know these techniques work. Coaches and shamans use positive reinforcement, affirmations, and visualizations to help people see what they might be and enable their efforts to move along that path.

Healing cultural mythologies

There is another level in which sensemaking is important for the shaman. In many traditional cultures shamans believe patients to be ill because there is something wrong with the narratives, cultural myths, or "stories" in the surrounding community. It is these myths or cultural narratives that the shaman attempts to heal, with the idea that healing the mythology will allow the patient to heal.[34] It is in the insight into and development of the new cultural narrative—new story, in a sense—that the sensemaking function of the shaman becomes important at the community, enterprise, or societal level, where so much positive change—healing—is desperately needed. Sensemaking is part of the leadership function of the shaman, even a spiritual leadership function. Sensemaking's main task is to help make sense of what is happening, i.e., to "make meaning" for others,[35] to tell a new story, develop new cultural mythologies, or change the narrative that explains life in some way.

Sensemaking, in a sense, is another instance of using imaginal thinking to create a new reality. It is what shamanic anthropologist Alberto Villoldo calls "dreaming the world into existence."[36] This sensemaking process is very much aligned with healing, for it is an effort to decrease dis-ease and dis-order, making new "sense" out of the situation. Much as we tell ourselves stories about how life has treated us and what we can expect individually, so whole cultures do much the same in the stories that tell us how the world works, what our "origin" was, and how we as human beings relate to the world around us.

In traditional cultures, shamans journey or travel imaginally or spiritually, often in trance, to different realms to gather new insights. Since these spiritual realms or other worlds are not accessible in ordinary states of consciousness, information can be found that helps to heal something that is amiss in the shaman's local culture. When local mythology has become disordered or dis-eased, creating disorder and disease in the person who is sick, in order to heal the patient the shaman must heal the community's mythology. To do that she or he needs information that can be found in different realms or worlds, i.e., the world of the spirits for the traditional shaman. For today's shamans, crossing intellectual, disciplinary, functional, organizational, and stakeholder-related boundaries can similarly provide significant insights that cannot be gathered in normal day-to-day bounded activities. But these new insights need a new story if they are to change the situation.

Drawing on locally developed and sometimes ancient practices, traditional shamans may engage in ceremonies, take consciousness-altering drugs, or engage in rituals such as drumming or dancing that induce trance states. They seek information from local spirits, guides, power animals, and the like, entities that makes sense in their cultural context, and bring back the new information, as shared by these entities, to the community. The stories that today's shamans construct need to be similarly resonant with local community language, existing stories and narratives, and the memes or core cultural artifacts that lie beneath them. For example, a failing company's leader might need to develop and share a new vision, hopefully collectively with others in the enterprise, if the organization is to move away from non-productive practices towards new ones that have better chance of success. Developing new visions, telling new stories, and creating new insights are all part of the sensemaking practice of the shamanic leader.

Sensemaking and the shamanic leader

Leaders as shamans inspire people to heal themselves, their organizations, and the broader communities and societies in which they live. Shamanic leaders inspire in part by reframing the cultural mythology of the community or organization in healthier, values-based directions, than those that may currently exist. In part, they use their power to help others open up to *their* own powers and walk through whatever sources of fear or resistance they might have so that they can tap into their own talents, energies, and generate new ideas, insights, and solutions to problems. Then they help others do much the same for themselves so that they can achieve their highest potential.

Leaders as shamans need not use rituals, magic, or drugs to achieve the shamanic state, in my view. They simply need to raise their own awareness of the system as it actually is through whatever means is feasible, tapping into that core knowledge that lies within each of us when we "see" clearly. As noted, such insights can be gained through meditation or related mindfulness practices, gaining insight through a wide variety of means including through other people or by reading, or by experiencing the system in non-typical ways.

Shamans need to attain a reasonable and realistic understanding of the system. Systems understanding is another of the elements associated with wisdom, along with aesthetic sensibility and moral imagination, used, as with shamanism, in the service of a better world. Then shamanic leaders focus on making better what is problematic, using whatever abilities they might have as healers, connectors, and sensemakers. They need to do these things with what Buddhists might call "right work" kept firmly in mind: that is, with the right intent oriented towards personal and systemic integrity. They do these things with a willingness to be open to intuition and guidance that seems to come from either deep within or from other sources. They need to keep in mind the desire to make the world a better place rather than serve selfish interests, which is the orientation of the negative shaman—the sorcerer.

Healing by itself is not enough to classify a leader as a shaman, since arguably most leaders want their enterprises to become better than they currently are, often by growing or making more money. Shamanic leaders, like traditional shamans, implicitly understand the importance of sensemaking, for part of leadership in our modern context is to help people find meaning in their work and organizations. Shamanic leaders can do this by articulating the purpose of the focal enterprise in ways that engender meaning and a sense of purpose. Most stakeholders even in businesses will not resonate much to a purpose that is articulated along the lines of maximizing shareholder wealth or growth for growth's sake. That type of reasoning is fundamentally aligned with materialistic values that are, in the end, quite shallow and do not provide a lasting source of meaning—sensemaking—for most people. Rather, the shamanic leader makes sense of his or her enterprise, organization, or group by finding and articulating a broader purpose: something that shows how the enterprise relates to the bigger picture and actually does "good" or "right work" in the world.

Traditional shamans work in part by helping community members understand what is wrong with the way the myths in their community are currently formulated—because they are of the belief that communities and their members get sick when the cultural mythology is out of alignment. Similarly, the sensemaking role of the shamanic leader is crucial in helping organizational members understand the broader purpose and function of their enterprise—as well as their own place within the enterprise and how they can contribute to achieving the purpose. It can also help people see how and where their particular enterprise fits into the broader community or society, as well as what the constructive (and negative) contributions are.

The connecting and sensemaking functions are important to shamanic leadership because shamans think and act holistically rather than in atomized or fragmented ways. Shamanic leaders within enterprises connect across disciplines, organizational functions, and other boundaries, including externally with different stakeholders interested in the enterprise's activities. They try to make the activities of the *whole* enterprise make sense to all these constituents as part of their sensemaking function. They bring people together to work collaboratively on projects so that the product or service being developed can be integrated across the necessary functions and tasks rather than fragmented into pieces that become hard to put together into an integrated whole.

The shamanic leader is able to talk with and understand the perspectives and points of view of many different stakeholders in shaping the vision, mission, and values of the enterprise. Because shamans tend to be seers, the shamanic leader is also good at envisioning an inspiring future for the enterprise—and bringing others along to help shape that vision. This seeing capability is an important element of leadership in general, recognized as vision, in part because it is in the vision of how the enterprise contributes to the world that purpose can be found. Purpose, as is becoming increasingly clear even in individual contexts,[37] is a core ingredient of healing—and it is the healing role that is central to the work of the shaman.

4

Answering your call to purpose

In this chapter, we explore what it takes to become a shaman in today's context. That is, this chapter covers how can we tap the out-of-ordinary experiences of the shaman and put them to good use in our work, relationships, and lives as we think about what our particular roles in healing the troubled world might be.

Answering *your* call to purpose

Intellectual and other types of shamans might not describe it this way, but it is clear from reviewing their life histories that, in some respects, they all answered a "call" to do the work that they ended up doing. In effect, they are answering a call to purpose that is uniquely theirs. Our own callings may guide us away from or towards traditional paths or careers. They might involve religion or spirituality—or might be secular. They might place us in the realm of doing whatever is "expected" of us by someone important to us. Or, the call to purpose might somehow prevent us from following all the implicit and sometime explicit "rules" that seem to guide many people in their career and life choice because we implicitly know that we need to be doing something else to fulfill our own sense of purpose.

What is crucial is that you answer the call to *your* purpose. That means doing enough reflection and becoming self-aware enough to know what it is to which you are called. Whether it is a certain type of work, hobby, or artistic endeavor, what we "must" do to serve the world is unique to each of us. It cannot be what our parents, mentors, or "society" in some manifestation wants us to do unless that is our own calling.

The idea of a "calling" is often associated with a call to a certain religion, to become a teacher or spiritual leader in that religion. The notion of calling, however, is actually much broader when it means a calling to whatever work, activities, activism, hobbies, artistic and creative endeavors, relationships, passionate pursuits, and particular interests really engage us and provide meaning in our lives. The idea of the calling is associated with our deepest passions and the purpose that we are "meant" to live out in this life. Answering the call to purpose is profoundly spiritual in the sense that it is purpose, and living out purpose, that gives meaning to our lives and helps us live purpose-filled lives.

Answering the call means delving deeply into whatever passions and purposes drive us, where we will be most fulfilled. For the shaman, it is discovering where we can make the most contribution based on whatever gifts we have and choose to develop. We all probably know people who simply wander through life doing pretty much what is expected of them by others without a lot of passion or deep engagement. Such people never really commit to something that fully engages them and seem to live life on the surface. They never seem to really engage with people, ideas, interests, work, or art that allows them to thrive and that somehow brings their particular form of healing into the world.

Following a calling is not necessarily easy. It can mean gaining expertise and mastery of a pursuit or type of work that requires demanding training, rigorous effort, and, simply, hard work. It can mean stepping away from what poet Robert Frost might have called the "road more travelled"[38] and going down that less-travelled road to find out what it is you are being called *to*. Sometimes, answering the call can take years of training, education, and passionate pursuit of knowledge, practice, learning, and insight. Following your calling can mean being willing to take a sometimes risky path towards achieving those purposes and passions, especially if what you are called to requires both high skill and talent and is in an area where few achieve top status. Doing so is not always the most lucrative route. It definitely means doing what *we* are called to do and not necessarily what others want us to do. It is not always what our parents, mentors, siblings, and friends want us to do, which is where courage and risk come into the process. Following our calling can sometimes take us to some pretty weird and unexpected (albeit fulfilling) places.

Your call to purpose can mean stepping into a place of great uncertainty and doubt, even when you feel compelled to go in that direction. It may be that you are called to do something that few others have attempted or that is outside your current knowledge area. In that case, finding like-minded others who are struggling with their own callings can be helpful, as can using various mindfulness and visioning techniques to help you figure out what to do. Sometimes, once you have started down a path, you realize that it is not right for you and recognize that it is time to shift gears to find a path more suited to your interests, talents, and sense of purpose. There can be fits and false starts to pursuing the call, a need to regroup, and sometimes change how you are going about things.

It is all too easy for others to try to impose their expectations, dreams, and desires on us, hoping that somehow we will fulfill *their* dreams, expectations, and desires. I see these expectations all the time in my home field of management education, where undergraduates are often told to major in what their parents believe will give them the best opportunities, whether or not they have affinity for those fields. For example, becoming an accountant because your parents think it is a good career, when you are not detail-oriented or sure that you like numbers much, can seriously distract you from finding your own calling.

The situation is evident in doctoral education in management disciplines, where I have been both a participant and observer for many years. Doctoral education is (in some ways like some forms of shamanism) an apprenticeship, in which students are socialized into the norms, values, and aspirations that their mentors have for themselves. In today's academic world, for example, there are often clear expectations for the nature, type, and number of publications that a successful academic will achieve, at least in my field of management. Deviating from these expectations by, for example, focusing on your passion for excellence in teaching or working directly with management practice through consulting, puts a young scholar outside the normal set of expectations for a successful academic career.

Expectations for many academics are rather narrowly constructed these days. To be "successful" as a scholar, for example, in my field of management increasingly requires publishing (a lot) in top-tier journals, paying relatively less attention to teaching and, indeed, even to the practice of management. This path is difficult enough on its own, even if that is the path to which you are called. It is that much more difficult if you happen to be someone called to teaching or working directly with businesses.

I am sure that similar expectations exist in all walks of life, whether for doctors, engineers, accountants, technicians, artists, plumbers, electricians, carpenters, nurses, therapists, or teachers, just to name a few. Following someone else's expectations or, for that matter, "society's" expectations is unlikely to provide a space for you to develop your shamanic insights and gifts. As a side, it is also not likely to make you very happy as a person either.

The question that must be asked is: "whose calling is this?" If it is truly yours, then it makes all kinds of sense to follow that path. However, if it is someone else's path imposed on you, then you need to dig deeply to find out what *your* actual calling is. Answering the call to shamanism thus means carving out your own niche, your own creative outlets, and your own approaches to your interests, work, and life.

Using your instincts and intuitions, creating quiet spaces for reflection—say, in meditation or through journaling—can be helpful in figuring out what your calling and purpose are. So can thinking about the places to which your attention is drawn and then, sometimes creatively, considering what types of jobs in those and related fields can provide a living. Sometimes you know you are on the right path towards your purpose when things suddenly start to seem aligned, when an opportunity presents itself to you that you might not have recognized previously but that somehow seems "right." Recognizing and being willing to pursue that intuition or instinct, to grab that opportunity, could mean pursuing a certain type of education, training, or apprenticeship, taking a new job, learning something new, pursuing an emerging interest, or some other appeal. When such opportunities arrive synchronistically—just when you need them—it can mean that you are drawing on the shaman's "out of the ordinary" experience.

Following the call, or your passion, is not always easy or the most lucrative path, so the choice is not always an easy one. For many people, however, I believe that following that internal call to do what is best for them will ultimately turn out to be what is best for the world because doing what they are called to do means they will best develop whatever gifts they have and best be able to serve the world. But to follow that call, you need the internal strength—indeed courage—to take the risks that are associated with following a different-from-the-expected path— even of *being* different themselves from your colleagues or co-workers.

There are two key insights here. Letting go of the expectations you have of others is difficult at best. Letting go of others' expectations of you is even harder. In the end, however, we must all find our own paths—to becoming the best shaman that we can be so that we can do whatever work it is that *we* are called to do to help heal the world.

Rebirth: dying to the old ways, awakening to the new

Becoming a shaman can be a trial for some people, particularly in the early stages, as the shaman experiences various difficulties that test his or her commitment to the path of healing. Discovering what your gifts are can be a part of this testing process. It can also lead to a rich and fulfilling life, but that does not mean there will not be obstacles and trials along the way. Initiation into shamanic ways can even require significant transformation of the self, sometimes a form of imaginal death and rebirth. Sometimes a serious illness, accident, or traumatic life event becomes a trigger for this transition. Sometimes insight comes in meditation or other practices. Sometimes it happens in a significant life transition when you need, in a sense, to reinvent yourself. In a sense, when the shaman receives the "call" to the healing path of shamanism, it is sometimes hard to ignore or, more importantly, is ignored at the peril, in a sense, of one's soul.

One thing that frequently happens to traditional shamans during their apprenticeships is an experience of dying to the old ways so that the new can emerge. Obviously, "real" death as we typically understand it is not the object here. Rather, the idea is that the shaman becomes someone new—someone more healed than previously—because (hopefully) harmful old ways, thoughts, and patterns have shifted. Eyes open, new awareness enters, purpose changes, and relationships shift. In such experiences, something happens that either profoundly or subtly changes who you are and how you are in the world. In a sense, a "new" person has been (re)born, typically out of some sort of struggle.

This imaginal death and rebirth process typically happens in an altered state of consciousness—the trance state discussed before. Although it can be difficult to imaginally witness your death—however you experience it—there is power in the sense of rebirth because it brings the suggestion that you can grow, learn, and change to become the person you need or want to be. One key in this process is dealing with—walking through—the fear that probably comes along with this experiences. You can generate these states for yourself in a meditative state of some sort if you are willing to try to stick with the attempt. Sometimes it may be helpful to have a guide, teacher, or friend with you during such an effort to help bring you back to ordinary reality if the situation becomes too difficult. However, this fear can be mitigated by knowing that the difference between imaginal realities and insanity is that you can return to everyday reality if you are of sound mind. (If you have experienced mental health problems, it is probably best if you do not attempt an imaginal experience of death and rebirth.)

This transition from the old to the new is a form of awakening, a sort of rebirth. It can be profound and fundamental, causing major life shifts relatively quickly, or much more subtle and occurring over a long period of time. We are each unique and our path to awakening, to finding our inner shaman, is going to be unique to our background, experience, and openness. In any case, this journey is part of becoming fully who you must be. It is, in essence, a journey into the innermost depths of yourself that allows discovery of your fundamental purpose(s) in life.

Traditional shamans might face this struggle in the passage through an illness, a life crisis, a vision quest, or other experience that fosters a new way of perceiving the world. Or there might be rituals and even drugs that cause them to experience their own vision, death, and rebirth or awakening. Native Americans, for example, often went on vision quests to find their personal vision, or even their rightful name, which often reflected their calling and purpose. Other types of rituals, such as ecstatic dance, drumming, chanting, and other trance-inducing practices, can facilitate such experiences. Today's shamans, of course, can use similar techniques if they wish to accelerate their journeys towards shamanism.

Sometimes, however, the rebirthing process almost seems accidental or, certainly, unplanned. For some people, there is a real-life near-death experience that sheds light on the old ways that the person has been using and causes him or her to shift. The transition might also occur because of significant life changes: for example, in today's world, the death of a loved one that causes you to reflect on what is really important, a divorce, job loss, or a similar experience that is upending in some way. Such experiences can cause you to rethink your life in important ways.

Other people experience an awakening to their own need to become the healer, connector, and/or sensemaker because of career change or a move to another part of the country or world. Awakening can also occur in the context of a relationship: for example, with a teacher who helps you see things differently, or with a loved one. Or it could be something that someone says, something that you see or read, that just gets you thinking and "seeing" differently, opens your eyes, and awakens you to new possibilities. For some, it might be an experience of either doing or observing art that opens them up to new possibilities and new ways of being in the world.

Some shamans come into their awareness and what I have called "being fully who they must be" through working with a teacher. Others undertake some form of apprenticeship in whatever modality or tradition appeals most to them, or perhaps several different modalities and traditions over time. Perhaps, as in traditional shamanic apprenticeships, they undertake a "journey" to spiritual (or other, e.g., artistic, disciplinary, systemic) realms, where they learn something new that becomes important to them. This learning can help them create a new vision for their purpose or way of being. Sometimes new awareness can come in a meditative state, a dream, or the more traditional trance-induced shamanic journey in which the initiate experiences something profound in their particular imaginal realms. Sometimes this rebirthing process can take place as a result of learning, spiritual inquiry or experiences, or psychological or other therapeutic means. In short, rebirth can take many forms, and what is right for you is just that: right for you.

What does this rebirth mean? Who are you in this new form? You may look pretty much as you always did, but there is something different about you, even if you are the only person who recognizes it. Maybe your purpose in life has become clearer. Maybe you are better able to relate to others. Maybe you have greater focus and concentration than before (or perhaps less). Maybe you have discovered some formerly hidden part of yourself that allows you to release creative energies that were previously suppressed. Maybe you find yourself acting differently in relationships, being able to relate to people better and more openly, or finding new insights as you explore your relationships. Maybe you find you can help others in new ways, e.g., helping them find their own insights or actually doing a type of "helping" work that connects you to people in a new way.

Perhaps you have new ideas, or can connect old ideas in different ways than you used to be able to do. Perhaps your artistic vision has matured and evolved to a new form. Perhaps you can relate to people, community, or nature in new and healing ways. Perhaps you make connections among people or ideas that others do not make. Perhaps you can help others see those connections. Possibly the rebirth that follows struggle can enable you to find your own path towards making a positive difference in the world. Each of us has something to offer and, by tapping into our inner shamans, we can help release that offering.

Many paths to becoming fully who you are

If I have learned anything from studying the academics I call intellectual shamans it is that we each have our own path to follow and that our lives as shamans (or otherwise) are best when we follow that path. The intellectual shamans had to, as I put it in the book, "become fully who they are," So, too, you need to become fully who *you* are in answering your own call to purpose. What that means is that you have to do the work, art, or relationships that only you can do in the interest of serving the world.

Answering the call to being shaman, as discussed above, is the first step in becoming fully who you are—as a person and as a shaman. What becoming fully who you are means in practice is following your own intuition, instincts, and motivations to shape the ways in which what you do helps heal the world around you. In a very real way, it means being the best you that you can be. There is a centeredness about most shamans that is notable, which I call the light that seems to exude from many such people. In part that centeredness comes from the practices that have helped them open up their awareness, i.e., various types of mindfulness and related practice. In part, it comes from simply knowing who they are—and living out who they are to the fullest.

Becoming fully who you are is probably a lifelong quest for most of us. It basically means following your own inner light, inner sources of power, and insights that come from honed intuition and instincts to do your best to make the world better. Being fully who you are in the shamanic sense typically has an element of giving to others or the world around you, of somehow going beyond the self. Note that the fulfillment of purpose that comes from this goes well beyond the sense of *homo economicus* or self-interested rationalizer which today's dominant economic narrative tells us is the core of human beings. Shamans cannot, by the nature of their work and the need to be healers, be entirely self-interested. Indeed, biology research has demonstrated that humans (and many other animals) are collaborative and cooperative as well as competitive, with self-interest existing alongside interest in others. Doing work simply for recognition, status, or financial gain, for example, does not really qualify as shamanic, even when that work has inadvertent benefits beyond the person.

Shamanic work is intentional and requires attention to something beyond the self for healing purposes. Ironically, it is exactly this going beyond self that allows "self" to come fully into being as you fulfill the purpose to which you have been called. Becoming fully who you are requires openness and awareness to what comes to you. It requires that sense of "allowing," which means accepting that what is, is what is and what it will be. Sometimes shamans need to recognize that they cannot change "what is." Other times, they know they are called to do exactly that: change what is. That is, sometimes being a shaman demands a recognition that we are sometimes called to change what is possible to change. Knowing which is which, what we can and should change and what needs to be accepted because it simply is, is key to being a shaman. Shamans, in addition to their holistic and healing orientation, sense of purpose, and open awareness, also have a willingness to take risks to follow their passion for whatever their healing work is. They have a willingness to engage deeply with self, others, and the world around them when that is needed, and boundless curiosity that results in ongoing, lifelong learning and development.

Shamanic people can sometimes feel as though they are rebels, mavericks, misfits, and outsiders. Frequently they do not fit neatly into already-designed positions, because they think differently, often more holistically and with greater insight, than many other people do, and they are "seeing around corners" or making connections that others do not. Sometimes their maverick status is because sometimes they can see through the "way things are done here" to a new way of doing things that makes people who are happy with the status quo uncomfortable. Some shamans in this sense can seem like trouble-makers or rabble-rousers in efforts to do their healing work, although others do their work quietly and with little fanfare.

Becoming fully yourself in the shamanic sense is not always an easy path. Your own call may take you along unexpected or unplanned routes, simply because you come to realize that the complexity of serving the world cannot necessarily be predicted in advance. Further, there is no one path to becoming fully who you are. All of us must do that in our own unique ways, with whatever resources and gifts we have. Sometimes, as discussed above, there is a trigger event that brings a new awareness of the non-ordinary experiences of life. Sometimes, the path is more direct and explicit, as when a would-be shaman undertakes training or education that enhances abilities and insights. Other times opportunities that lead people to shamanic experiences arise—and are taken advantage of. Sudden or chronic illness, the death of a loved one, career transitions, layoffs, exposure to new people and interests, and any number of other events can lead you towards the shamanic path.

The great mythologist Joseph Campbell called the transition to a shamanic path a "shamanic crisis." He claimed that whatever the crisis, i.e., the imaginal experience of "death and rebirth," represents a form of "threshold initiation." This initiation, whatever form it takes, helps the shaman shift to a much broader perspective, i.e., from whatever communities she or he is already in to the universe and, arguably, the universal aspects of spirit accessed in non-ordinary reality and then used for healing purposes. This aspect of the shaman's path, an element of what Campbell called the hero's quest, a universal rite of passage across cultures, he believed, resulted in individuals that are physically healthier with greater stamina, are more vital of spirit, and are more intelligent than those typical of whatever group the shaman comes from.[39] The insight here is that there are many paths to becoming a shaman. You need to follow the one that works for you. Similarly, as the next section articulates, shamans have many different types of gifts with which to do their work.

Gifts of the shaman

Each shaman has and uses a gift or set of gifts. Others' gifts will be not necessarily be the same as yours. After you are called to shamanism, you need to "allow" (because you can't force) your particular shamanic gifts to become evident. Then you need to develop your gift and be willing to use it appropriately and for healing, connecting, and sensemaking purposes with the greater good kept constantly in mind. Since I believe that we all have the capacity to become shamans, we need to tap into our deepest inner resources, walking through the fear associated with becoming fully who we must be. That can be a scary thing, since, as discussed earlier, the path is not always straight or expected. Then we need to follow whatever healing path is needed for ourselves, so that we can use our powers for healing others and the world around us, allowing the universe (by whatever name you give it) to help you open up to the possibilities that are available for you.

Some people's gifts are pretty much what you might imagine when you think of the shaman: the power to see, feel, or otherwise experience energy, spirit, or other things in the world in some alternative way from day-to-day experience. Some shamans say they have the power to see, hear, or otherwise experience spirits or other beings beyond the normal realm. They might even have what some would label psychic powers that allow a wide range of intuitive experiences and insights not available to most of us in our everyday reality. Some shamans sense and use energy. They can perform energy healings, for example. I believe that many people who use energy-based healing techniques, such as acupuncture, reiki, healing hands, vibrations, bodywork, hypnosis, soul retrieval, and other so-called alternative forms of healing (alternative approaches to Western style medicine, that is) which are less familiar in our modern context, are serving shamanically. In effect, they are living out their particular way to help heal the world or others.

Shamanism in today's context, then, is partially about working with whatever gifts you have. Over the years I have come to know people with a variety of gifts. Some of these gifts appear to have supernatural or metaphysical elements. Many are grounded in intuition or everyday reality. Some shamans focus predominantly and explicitly on healing people of diseases (dis-eases) or other dis-orders, perhaps by working in a medical field or as a therapist or counselor, where healing is the centerpiece of their work. In such work what might be called intuitive insights—derived perhaps from the ability to connect across ideas or gather insights from inner or universal sources—become evident.

Many shamanic individuals are energy healers, acupuncturists, or are working with other alternative forms of medicine that explicitly use energy to help with healing. Even when a healer does not consider him- or herself to be a shaman, various shamanic functions can be tapped: for example, through gifted diagnostic or interpersonal skills that help patients begin to heal themselves, through ecological or entrepreneurial insights, or through inventiveness of various kinds. Other shamanically oriented people, for example, claim to see "souls" of people who have passed over. Others hear messages from these souls or from the universe (or what they might call God, Spirit, or spirits, including so-called power animals). Still others can "see" what is going on with others, and enhance their experiences. Some can create needed "space" around people or for an issue to emerge simply by sitting and "being."

Still others who work with energy for healing purposes can seemingly direct that energy. Others connect across a variety of types of boundaries to generate insights, knowledge, or "knowings" that are useful to themselves or others. Others have the gift of insight and intuition, and are able to use that gift to help others make sense of their situation, themselves, their communities, their relationships, or the world about them. Some people use their shamanic gifts as artists, for example, in drawings or paintings, photography, dance, music, writing, storytelling, poetry, sewing, knitting, and creative hobbies of different kinds, or other artistic endeavors. In doing so, they bring joy, meaning, and spirit into their own and others' lives, which is fundamentally a healing function. The creative capacity is certainly an important shamanic gift, since we really have very little idea where creative inspirations come from.

Still other people use their gifts by leading others, whether in business enterprises or other types of institutions. Some are activists, working in the world for change. Some are organizational development specialists and change agents. Some are social or conventional entrepreneurs, wanting to bring new products and services that can help the world to life. There is no limit to the ways in which shamanic gifts can be put to use.

Shamans effectively help to create meaning and insight in a wide variety of ways, using their instincts, intuitions, and deep insights to make connections that others are not making. Through the sensemaking function, they help others create meaning in the work that they do, in their relationships, and in the world around them. It is clear that shamans can use very different gifts in doing their work through the three main activities or functions of the shaman—healing, connecting, and sensemaking. Because my "gift," such as it is, is that of connecting across ideas, and sometimes people, and integrating them, it has been hard for me to accept that I was actually on a shamanic path. This difficulty in accepting what my shamanic working group has told me over the years has also, in the end, led to my current belief (or maybe insight) that everyone has and can use shamanic healing in life if they are willing to accept whatever gift it is that they have been given and put it to good use.

Practice: there is no one way

People often want to know *how* to become more shamanic in their lives. I believe that some sort of regular practice is necessary. In my view that practice needs to be reflective, meditative, or mindfulness-oriented. Mindfulness practices of various sorts help you can get away from the turmoil of daily life to access the inner wisdom or, as psychologist Carl Jung would have called it, the collective unconscious. Traditional shamans would call these practices journeying to the spiritual realms.

Many teachers and so-called gurus will try to tell you that their way is the right or even *only* way to gain the kinds of insights that shamans need to do their work. I don't think that is true, and neither does my teacher. Although some sort of reflective, meditative, or mindfulness practice is probably needed, there are any number of approaches that you can use to gain the wisdom needed to become a shaman who exercises the roles of healer, connector, and sensemaker in the service of a better world. The practice that is best for you is, as with any form of exercise or practice, the one that you will actually *do* on a regular basis.

Over the years, for example, I have read many books and participated in John Myerson's "Way of Power" group. Through these activities and some other participatory events, I have learned and adapted a number of techniques that I have used in my own (almost daily) practice. These practices seem to work for me, but they may be quite different from the ones that work for you. I do think, however, that some sort of regular practice is necessary. Since I firmly believe that there is no "one right way" to become and be a shaman, I think it is up to each of us to use whatever approaches and techniques appeal—and that we can regularly use.

My own approach to practice was strongly influenced initially by George Leonard and Michael Murphy's *The Life We Are Given: A Long-Term Program for Realizing the Potential of Body, Mind, Heart and Soul*.[40] Then later it was reinforced by Ken Wilber's, Terry Patten's, Adam Leonard's, and Marco Morelli's concept of "integral life practice.[41] Both of these integral approaches argue that we need practices that address the complex interactions of mind, body, heart, and spirit/soul. For me an integral practice means doing a great deal of reading, writing, reflection, and thinking as a mind-based practice. It also means adopting and adapting a combination of (relatively easy-going) tai qi and yoga exercises for the body practice. For the heart practice, I worked individually with my teacher, John Myerson, where I had to learn to open my heart, be aware of my emotions, and develop better relationships with people (moving away from the "tough" stance I had taken earlier in life). During this time and with the Way of Power group I had to learn to recognize a deep sadness (in my case) that needed to be acknowledged and then let go.

That emotional connection was aided by reflective practices associated with particular forms of body work. Such practices allow for concentrated attention, and various forms of meditation and journeying imaginally, which are part of the spirit/soul work. In addition, as part of the heart and spirit/soul work, I began to play my guitar again, eventually joining singing groups, going to music camp for the folk music I love, and beginning to both write and play out my own songs, sometimes alone and sometimes with others. This heart and soul work has immeasurably enriched my life and enables me to "give back" in a variety of ways beyond my work as a professor and scholar. These approaches, along with the Way of Power group, have allowed me to access and "hold" emotions, creativity for my writing and scholarship, and, I hope, to generally become calmer and more centered. In addition, I have been able to open up in new ways to people, ideas, and connections that need to be made. The particular things I do have shifted and evolved over time, as you might expect your own practice and approaches to do.

What you need to develop for your practices, however, is up to you, based on what you need and what appeals to you. Some form of meditative, mindfulness, or reflective practice helps provide the mental "space" to allow access to and insight from the non-ordinary events that happen to all of us, but which we too often do not notice. My practices work for me but are unlikely to work as well for someone else, because I designed them for my particular interests and needs. Part of the task of "becoming shaman" is developing cognitively at least to the stage that developmental psychologist calls "self-authoring."[42] Self-authoring means you are able to rely on your own intuitions, instincts, and assessments to do what is right for you rather than always needing someone else's guidance; though at least at first some guidance from the proper teacher can be very helpful, as it was in my case.

Of course, in addition to some form of mindfulness practice, we also have to do the analytical and inquiry work necessary to gain expertise and knowledge in areas where such learning is important. Practices that quiet the mind and provide a "space" for insight, connections, and deep experiences of non-ordinary reality to emerge are vitally important for the shaman's insight—accessing what, in other words, is beyond the rational, analytical, and immediately empirically observable. Insight meditation, meditations using a koan or Buddhist puzzle, meditations where you empty your mind, meditations on specific subjects, ideas, problems, or issues, loving-kindness meditations, and guided mediations, among other forms of meditative practice, can all be helpful. Similarly, using traditional techniques like drumming, chanting, toning, dancing, for journeying to what Indigenous shamans call spiritual realms and Jung called the collective unconscious, can provide for that space that generates understanding.

Meditation and mindfulness practices and trance states are really about focused awareness. Such practices come from any number of traditions and are not necessarily associated with any particular one, though many of us are familiar with Buddhist approaches that advocate different meditative practices. Meditative practices generally help to build the capacity for attention and concentration, for mindfulness, which simply means being present in *this* moment rather than having your mind wander (as minds do) all over the place, and for opening your heart and soul to what is, which we can call compassion—for yourself, for others, and for the world around us. Meditation and mindfulness approaches can help you reduce stress, better connect to yourself and others, improve your focus, and generally calm you down so that you are not as "reactive" to situations and other people as you might have been.

Everyone can meditate or practice mindfulness. It need not take up hours of your day (although, for some yogis and shamans, it does). Just five minutes of some sort of meditative practice, like sitting quietly while focused on your breath, an image, an idea, or a word, for example, can be helpful in getting you started if you do not already have a practice. You will find that your practice evolves as you begin to learn more about it and as the need arises—and as you gain greater insight. As with traditional shamanic practices and techniques, there are any number of books or online resources that can provide specific details about how to engage in meditative and mindfulness practices. Or you can find a teacher whose approach fits your needs. Alternatively, you can use recorded, online, or in-person guided meditations, which are a form of journeying, if that approach makes the most sense for you. In any case, I would urge you to consider adopting at least one of them that fits into your lifestyle.[43]

Some physical practices like yoga, tai qi, qi gong, and some martial arts have elements of and can help develop mindfulness as well as being good for your body. Such practices can provide helpful ways to bring yourself into the moment and enhance awareness, which is partly what gaining insight is all about. Simply learning to be present in this moment, now, attentive to others and really "with" them can be forms of meditative practice that allow for insights. Moments of insight can also happen in the context of relationships or working in teams with others if you fully engage with the other, putting your focus and attention on him or her while, in a sense, "losing" your own self and needs for that period of time.

For some people, the best way to gain insights will be traditional shamanic journeying—traveling imaginally to spiritual realms to collect information. You can then bring it back for healing purposes—at whatever level of analysis is appropriate for the work you do—individual, group, organizational, or even broader in the world. Shamanic journeying means using your imaginative powers in altered states of consciousness to "travel" to other, typically spiritual, realms, visit with the powers, spirits, and generate insights that you find there, and bring what you learn back.

In addition to accessing their inner resources or the collective unconscious, today's shamans can experience realm-crossing by integrating different disciplines together, by crossing organizational, sector, or functional boundaries, by working at what I sometimes call the "interstices" of organizations—the boundaries either with or to the external world. Sometimes they can engage these types of awareness-enhancing activities by working or being with people who are very different from themselves, who bring different ideas and perspectives to conversations, relationships, practices, and actions. While these types of activities may not induce the trance states typical of shamanic journeying, when awareness is opened up through mindfulness, they can provide opportunities to exercise and engage the connecting function of the shaman. Such experiences can be out of the ordinary because they expose you to different ideas, ways of thinking, practices, and ways of being in the world than simply staying in one realm can do.

Trance states and shamanic journeys can be induced through meditative and reflective practices that allow your mind to stop obsessing about worries, day-to-day concerns, and the constant internal conversation that most of us have inside our heads most of the time. Drumming, dancing, singing, chanting, and other repetitive methods induce this trance state. Some Indigenous shamans use drugs of various sorts to induce the trance state, although such techniques are not necessarily the only way to induce the openness to new experiences, insights, and awareness that trance (hypnotic or altered states of consciousness, as they are often known) can bring about.

Trance is much the same thing as what the psychologist Mihály Csíkszentmihályi calls "flow" or sometimes "getting into the zone."[44] Csíkszentmihályi argues the flow state can be reached in any number of ways that engage you fully, challenge you somewhat, and create enjoyment: work and hobbies that demand focus and attention either through physical involvement (e.g., running and the "runner's high"), teamwork, demanding and engaging activities like making music, painting, drawing, writing, or other creative pursuits, or any practice that you pay attention to intensively, and where you get immediate feedback about how well you are doing. Similar activities can induce this state of flow, which Csíkszentmihályi argues is a core part of a happy life. During the state of flow, as in trance, time seems to disappear, the full engagement is a very enjoyable experience of vitality and presence in the moment, and the person can lose consciousness of the self because attention is drawn to the relevant activity. Flow experiences are intrinsically rewarding—in other words, you don't need to be paid to do them (though when work creates flow, that can be a benefit!).

You can also think of the shaman's altered state of consciousness or trance as a form of hypnosis in which you are able to tap into deep internal reservoirs of wisdom and in some ways have the types of experiences that allow you to open to new things. For the shaman, however, simply going into a trance, hypnotic, or flow state is insufficient, because the shaman as healer, connector, and sensemaker needs to take the insights gained during these experiences and somehow use them for healing purposes. Here is one way to think about how personal meditative insights, flow, or trance experiences can help others. Such trance, hypnotic, or flow experiences can enhance a person's ability to be peaceful, calm, happy, and energized—and because we now know from psychological research that emotions are contagious, spreading to others around us, such states of contentment and happiness can help others around us to move towards similar states.[45]

In addition, you can use trance or hypnosis purposefully to help you find information that you need or be able to open up to new paths. For example, I often meditate on writing work that I need to do, asking that when I come back from the meditative state that I will be able to move forward on whatever work it is that needs to be done. Frequently, the insights, framing, and inspiration that I need is right there when I start to write again. Such "requests" of your inner self, the collective unconscious, or Spirit, however you frame it, can be helpful when you need motivation, insight, and inspiration and take the time to give yourself some space to reflect, journey to wisdom sources, and "bring back" what is needed.

The sensemaker role of shamans is, in a sense, one of spiritual leadership, according to Peter Frost and Carolyn Egri.[46] As sensemakers and on the individual levels, as an example, people with shamanic insights can help others understand, perhaps, what it means to be peaceful and at one with self, other, and the universe, much as good priests, therapists, and healers do. Of course, such experiences can also generate deep insights, even wisdom, when people reach into themselves and/or the collective unconscious[47] to bring back insights that they might not have otherwise generated—and are willing to share those insights productively with others.

5

Balance and harmony in self and the world

A foundational part of being a shaman is achieving balance and harmony. Harmony is needed in interpersonal relationships, within the relevant communities, and within individuals, including the shaman him- or herself. Balance and harmony are important in all relationships, especially, these days, in humans' relationship with the natural world around us, which has gone wildly out of balance. Some cultures believe that practicing shamanism is actually a way of life—an approach to living that focuses on harmony and balance between humans and all of the beings, including, sometimes, beings we might consider non-living, and manifestations of nature like rocks, lakes, rivers, mountains, and landscapes. As Serge Kahali King, who wrote *Urban Shaman*, notes, ". . . a shaman is a healer of relationships: between mind and body, between people and circumstances, between humans and Nature, and between matter and spirit."[48]

Despite the particularity of some shamanic systems, there are common elements that most shamans and shamanic practices share. As noted in the previous chapter, traditional shamans typically enter altered states of consciousness, i.e., trance states, in order to access different realms and bring back information. Often this information is in the form of new or different energy, or information from visions or "spirits" that helps the shaman "see" the situation facing his or her patient or the community in new ways. The idea of "seeing" is also a core shamanic attribute, although "seeing" does not always mean seeing visually but can mean experiencing, "knowing," feeling, hearing, or sensing the relevant information in some other way.

Indeed, because shamans are fundamentally healers when they draw from the deep spiritual reserves that are accessible to us all, we can say that people are exercising their shamanic power when they tap "non-ordinary" reality to improve relationships of all sorts, using intuition, instincts, creative insights, trance, or other means that go beyond simple analytical tools. Many of the world's most iconic figures could readily be considered to be shamans. Well-known figures with a healing orientation include religious notables like Christ, Confucius, and the Buddha, and we might well also put Gandhi and Martin Luther King into the category of shaman.

The connecting role of the shaman is most centrally a boundary-spanning role, which some scholars think of as "mediating realities."[49] Today, we sometimes think of mediating realities in the context of computer technologies that enable us to perceive something—a game, a world, a device—as if it were real by using wearable technological devices. For shamans, however, the idea means entering worlds that are typically invisible, and crossing boundaries to gain insight, ideas, ways of being or practicing that others typically do not access.

As I have noted earlier, shamans today can be found in just about any realm of experience or line of work that you can think of. Although they may or may not explicitly "journey" in the trance state as traditional shamans do, today's shamans do typically have to journey in some respect to gain the insights and information that they need. Where, for example, does the insight for healing of the gifted therapist, nurse, or physician come from? Is it simply derived from experience or education? Or does it come from a capacity to make connections and "see" the situation in ways that others do not, from some source deep within or beyond the self, because the person has opened up to different possibilities?

Some chess masters are said to be able to "see" the whole board with both past and forward moves simultaneously present, knowing through vast experience the ways in which the game can progress.[50] Similarly, shamans see situations holistically and understand their past and future dynamics, in order to work intuitively in journeying, whether to spiritual realms, across disciplines, institutions, or sectors, or bridging among different peoples and ideas, allowing information to come from whatever sources seem relevant. The shaman integrates information on the basis of experiences from a wide range of different situations or boundaries that have been crossed in the past, which can hopefully shed light on the new situation in new ways.

Not all of today's shamans enter the trance state quite as deliberately as do traditional shamans. There is a sense in which today's shaman may also be acting in trance, where the trance state somehow allows insights, ideas, and wisdom to come together in new ways in a given moment. The "flow" state as discussed above describes a trance state that many creative individuals in all walks of life enter into when they are working or otherwise acting at their peak; and, when things are going well, this state simply seems to happen.[51] The state is one in which time seems to disappear and individual in flow is focused entirely on the task at hand: that is, the person is completely absorbed in what is going on at that moment. The person's ego disappears into the task or experience and there is simply a state of "being" in this moment with whatever is happening. This state is very similar, if not identical, to the trance or hypnotic state and can open up the person to great creativity and insight. Such insights can appear intuitive and highly innovative, providing a holistic yet focused sense of the task, relationship, or whatever the object of flow is.

I believe that when modern shamans gain insights by crossing a range of boundaries, they have "let go" of their ego and are able to integrate numerous past experiences. That is when they are in this state of flow. The flow state allows past experiences and deep internal wisdom, perhaps drawn from the collective unconscious,[52] to become relevant as needed in the situation— and provide the type of holistic insight that the chess master experiences when looking at the chess board and envisioning what is likely to happen next. It is this openness to the present moment while simultaneously integrating relevant past experiences that, in my view, creates the insight that modern shamans exhibit in whatever their walk of life.

Spirituality and the shaman

Shamanism is said to be the world's oldest set of spiritual traditions. Prehistoric records frequently contain shamanistic images, suggesting that shamanism has been around since the earliest days of humanity. Shamans in traditional cultures believe that everything in the world around them is imbued with spirit: in effect, that everything has spirit or, we might say, life, including animals and plants, of course, but extending that view to things that most modern Western people would say are not living, like rocks, lakes, mountains, and rivers. We will explore this idea in more depth below.

Because of the pervasiveness of these beliefs, it is hard to avoid a conversation about spirituality when considering shamans, The connecting that traditional shamans do involves traveling on shamanic journeys to spiritual or other-worldly realms, rather than the more worldly or mundane realms in which we live day to day. In this sense, shamanism involves anything that is accessed or learned from non-ordinary reality via intuitions, instincts, deep meditations and trance states, or in seemingly ordinary states that open us up to making connections that we don't otherwise see. While many shamanistic people have created religions, shamanism itself is more a spiritual orientation than a particular religion, particularly because different cultures have different traditions, rituals, and beliefs. The shaman in a sense opens his or her awareness to possibilities, while maintaining a sense of awe about the wealth of those possibilities, about nature, and about others. The core elements of healing, connecting, and sensemaking, as well as a spiritual orientation, characterize the shaman, wherever found.

The physicist Fritjof Capra, writing with Pier Luigi Luisi, makes a clear distinction between spirituality and religion, which is relevant here, stating:

> Spirituality is a much broader and more basic human experience than religion. It has two dimensions: one going inward, or "upward," as it were; and the other going

outward, embracing the world and our fellow human
beings. Either of the two manifestations may or may not be
accompanied by religion.[53]

Spirituality, so differentiated, has everything to do with a
focus on the mysteries of the universe, of life itself, with the awe
with which the shaman approaches life and all of its manifestations. Spirituality in this sense involves developing the meaning
that we as humans apply to the world and to others, with
emphasis on doing "good" in the world whatever that means by
one's own lights. Indeed, Capra and Luisi highlight the work of
Gandhi and Martin Luther King as what they call the "lay spirituality" that exists with no need for a specific religious tradition.

Many of today's shamans exhibit various forms or aspects of
traditional of religious spirituality. They can and often are associated more with this "lay spirituality" in their search for meaning. In a sense, they are all about bettering and healing some
aspect of the world that is relevant to them, more than aligning
with particular religious traditions, although shamans can practice just about any denominational religion and still be shamanic. When I studied both intellectual shamans and difference
makers, for example, some had explicit religious beliefs, and
others were grounded in various spiritual traditions. Still others
expressed no particular spirituality except their deep search for
understanding and meaning within their work. Yet all were
doing work that used the three functions of healing, connecting,
and sensemaking to make the world a better place, which is how
today's shamans operate.

Indeed, the type of spirituality associated with shamanism is
akin to what psychologist Abraham Maslow called "peak experiences,"[54] and, as noted above, what Mihály Csíkszentmihályi

calls "flow."[55] Jon Kabat-Zinn, along with many practitioners of certain types of Buddhism, calls this state "mindfulness,"[56] which we considered as part of becoming a shaman in the last chapter. In peak and flow moments, attention is concentrated, the person is highly alert and aware of what is going on, while having little sense of "self" or ego, though there is a sense of being fully alive. As Capra and Luisi note, this sense of awareness is fully embodied and provides a deep sense of connection with the universe or with the "whole" of what is.

It is this connection that allows the shaman to delve into other realms. Sometimes these realms are spiritual realms.[57] Traditional shamans, for example, frequently speak of the lower, middle, and upper worlds, where the middle world is our experienced reality. Knowledge and information needed for healing purposes can be gathered by exploring these realms in the process of journeying, which involves entering a trance state and traveling imaginally to other, typically spiritual, realms to gather insight and information. In more modern terminology, these "other realms" are what psychologist Carl Jung called the "collective unconscious," the source of information tapped by shamans, for example through meditation techniques.

Capra and Luisi clearly outline the nature of the spirituality that shamans experience, although they are not explicitly alluding to shamans. They state, "Spiritual experience—the direct, nonintellectual experience of reality in moments of heightened aliveness—is known as a mystical experience because it is an encounter with mystery."[58] Such an "experience of a profound sense of connectedness, of belonging to the cosmos as a whole, . . . is the central characteristic of mystical experience," and is typically described as ineffable—unable to be articulated.[59]

Connectedness can come with insights gained by shamans by crossing normal boundaries and barriers, through journeying while in trance states, or by engaging in other awareness-enhancing practices. Albert Einstein in *The World As I See It* perhaps most famously articulated the sense of mystery and awe at the mystery of the universe that the shaman experiences in one way or another manifests. Though Einstein is writing without explicit reference to shamans, he could be speaking about today's shaman's sense of awe and wonder at what the intuitive mind can reveal when awareness is enhanced:

> The fairest thing we can experience is the mysterious. It is the fundamental emotion which stands at the cradle of true art and true science. . . . It was the experience of mystery—even if mixed with fear—that engendered religion. A knowledge of the existence of something we cannot penetrate, of the manifestations of the profoundest reason the most radiant beauty, which are only accessible in their most elementary forms—it is this knowledge and this emotion that constitute the truly religious attitude; in this sense, and in this alone, I am a deeply religious man. . . . Enough for me the mystery of the eternity of life, and the inkling of the marvelous structure of reality, together with the single-hearted endeavor to comprehend a portion, be it never so tiny, of the reason that manifests itself in nature.[60]

Indeed, Capra and Luisi speculate that it is this very sense of awe at the wonders and majesty of the universe that may have been humankind's first spiritual experience, experiences that are typically associated with the shaman.

In defining shamans as seers, visionaries, and individuals oriented to healing, making connections across realms, and making sense of those connections in the healing process in the service of a better world (community), it is clear that great religious leaders of many persuasions can be considered shamans. Christ, the Buddha, Mohammed, and Confucius certainly had these orientations in their work. Arguably, many more "ordinary" people who use the powers of seeing across boundaries and making sense of what they see to help heal the world, in their own ways also serve the role of modern shaman.

Shamanic wisdom

Today's shaman is not, as I have discussed, necessarily embedded deeply in the mythical or magical stories and structures of the past, though it can sometimes be helpful to learn some of stories, rituals, and practices associated with traditional practices. Indeed, many people find it comforting to adopt the rituals and traditions of some form of traditional shamanism when that works for them and they can find and connect to their spirit guides, power animals, rituals, rites, and ceremonies. For others in today's world, however, who are imbued with scientific understandings and "rational" thought (like me, for example), and who may live in urban settings not closely connected to nature, such traditional approaches may work less well.

Here is what I have learned: Being shamanic does not *necessarily* mean engaging in rituals or archaic practices, although these practices are helpful to some people. What it does mean is working with the gifts, energies, and responsibilities that you have to do whatever healing work you are called to. It means recognizing that not everything that is worth knowing can be known through rational analysis and scientific methodologies. Sometimes intuition, meditative techniques and associated altered states or consciousness, gut feelings, hunches, or "knowings," creative impulses, or other sources of inspiration that allow you to see or learn something that cannot be rationally explained are also valid ways of knowing and learning. Such insights and impulses are at the core of the shamanic experience. Becoming a shaman in a very real way means gaining and using wisdom that comes from these insights and creative surges in the service of the world, for I believe that the attributes of the shaman are similar to those of the wise person.

As we have seen, the work of the shaman in making the world, a community, or a person better, involves three sets of interrelated skills: healing, connecting, and sensemaking. Healing what is within one's power to heal can be directed at the individual, community, or even broader level. Healing means that you are focused on doing what you can do to bring about positive and constructive change that helps dissipate fear and bring "love" in all of its many meanings into that context. Healing is enhanced through the work of connecting. Connecting can take place across with another person or in groups of people, across different realms, disciplines, or other boundaries, or, in the context of spiritual realms, as with traditional shamans, who travel to different realms to gather and bring back relevant information, insights, and ideas for healing purposes. Sensemaking is the attribute of the visionary in some sense, spelling out how things are in understandable ways or envisioning the future compellingly: that is, making sense of what has been learned for others.

The late South African activist and former president Nelson Mandela, who has now passed on, was most likely a shaman. Mandela in 2007 convened a group of senior statesmen, activists, and human rights advocates called The Elders, a group that continues to meet. The Elders are senior statesmen and -women, who no longer hold public office and hence are independent actors. They work collectively on issues related to peace and human rights. They are leaders whose earlier work was as peace makers and peace builders, social revolutionaries, and pioneering women who headed up their governments, or former officials whose work involved social justice, human rights, and climate change, among other major global issues.[61] In addition to Mandela, the initial group of Elders included Kofi Annan (former Secretary-General of the United Nations), Jimmy Carter (former US president), Graça Machel (Mozambican politician and humanitarian), Mary Robinson (former UN High Commissioner for Human Rights), Muhammad Yunus (founder of Grameen Bank and related entities), Desmond Tutu (South African social rights activist and retired bishop), and Li Zhaoxing (former foreign minister of China), among others.

Respected for the work they have done in the world, The Elders can certainly be considered among the sages of today's world. The sage is someone, man or woman, who is venerated because of past experience, judgment, and wisdom, someone who is profoundly wise: that is, a wise elder. We live today in a world where the wisdom of the sage is sorely needed, yet in many cultures where elders, who might be expected to be considered wise resources by others, are ignored or shunted aside.

In most traditional communities, it is the shamans who are the wise persons, the sages to whom the community looks when advice, healing, or insight is needed that cannot be found in the normal course of events. Like The Elders, they are sought out when there are questions about the community, when there is dis-order or dis-ease, and when things need to change. In that sense, the shaman is a change agent—helping individuals and communities to heal. Mandela brought together The Elders to do their healing on a world stage and, in my view, there is much need of such wisdom to be brought to bear on our troubled systems, political organizations, and natural environment today.

By inferences, we can suggest that today's shamans in a sense are the wise elders who can through their sensemaking function somehow speak in ways that allow themselves and others to be heard. Sometimes they speak in ways that get others to actually listen and begin to change. Sometimes they create new language—memes or basic units of culture like ideas, images, phrases, and symbols[62]—that help others see the world in new ways. New memes can help people break away from old, dysfunctional ways of seeing, being, and interacting in the world. Such shamans may be scientists, writers, journalists, or academics who have figured out a way to translate their healing work so that non-scientists can readily understand. They may be healers, who work with energy or allopathic medicine. They may be therapists whose insights help people heal wounds inflicted by life or by others. They may be natural scientists whose work is oriented toward making the world a better place. They can even be politicians, like Mandela and former US president Jimmy Carter, who bring their wisdom and political sensibility to bringing about a better, more peaceful and sustainable world. They may be artists who see the world differently from most people of their time, providing new images and insights through their art.

Not all shamans are of an age to be called an elder; however, many people whom we might classify as *wise* elders have the traits of the modern shaman. They are, in short, healers, connectors, and sensemakers, who help us make better sense of our troubled world and can provide a guiding light for those in need. These three attributes of shamanism suggest to me that the shamanic process has a clear relationship to wisdom and to the process of becoming wise, recognizing that even wise people are imperfect and need to continue to grow and learn. Wisdom, in my view, is the capacity to use moral imagination, systems understanding, and aesthetic sensibility, as shamans do, in the service of a better world.[63]

Note first that both shamans and wise people work in the service of a better world at whatever scope is within their purview—individual, family, community, organization, or broader, sometimes even globally. Think, for example, of how Nelson Mandela's presence in South Africa during and after the Apartheid era has set an example for the entire world, or how Gandhi and Martin Luther King did much the same in their countries.

Wisdom's emphasis on moral imagination[64] highlights the central role of recognizing that there are ethical and values-related consequences embedded in all situations. From the perspective of moral imagination, there is no such thing as an "amoral" decision or context, for some set of principles, values, norms, or ethical consequences are embedded in all situations where we have an effect or impact. Moral imagination is a core aspect of wisdom because it represents the capacity to recognize those ethical and values-laden issues that are inherent in a given context. It is through the recognition of such ethical, values-related, and normative issues, along with systems understanding and aesthetic sensibility, that the shaman, often the wise elder in a community, can begin to understand what it is that needs to be healed. Such moral imagination is also integral to the shaman, whose work must be imbued with ethics because it inherently involves power.

Systems understanding, the second aspect of wisdom, involves the capacity to understand the system not in its fragments but as a whole and to know that there are consequences likely to ensue depending on what happens within the system. Of course, many systems are highly complex. No one, not even the wisest person in the world, will understand all aspects of the system or all consequences of a given action or decision. What is important is taking a holistic perspective of the system, rather than breaking it down into its component parts, and attempting to understand how the whole system will be changed or affected when actions and decisions are made.[65] As with moral imagination, the shaman needs systems understanding—a holistic perspective of the situation—to begin the healing process, and we have already seen how important this holistic understanding is to the work of the shaman.

Systems understanding can also involve the connecting function of the shaman because a holistic approach to a person, family, community, organization, or the world invariably means working across multiple functions, abilities, disciplines, and sub-systems. It is the ability to "connect" across different disciplines, realms, functions, and the like that characterizes the connecting function of the shaman, as well as the wise person.

The third aspect of wisdom, less well understood, is a creative element—it is aesthetic sensibility, which means understanding the design or aesthetic (or beauty-related) qualities of the system, action, decision, or practice. This capability of the wise person is also part of healing—as well as sensemaking. As we have said, when shamans do their healing, they are attempting to bring order back from a dis-ordered or dis-eased world. It is exactly this dis-order and dis-ease that makes a decision, action, or situation lack beauty or an aesthetically pleasing quality. Because the central function of the shaman is in bringing such order and ease into place—for example, by telling the community a new story that enables the patient to heal—aesthetic sensibility to reshape the story, the art, the design as relevant to the situation becomes vitally important.

The world desperately needs more shamans, more elders, even more witches, wizards, magicians, and clowns, who bring these attributes of moral imagination, systems understanding, and aesthetic sensibility into their work every day, who are wise even beyond their years. Elders and the wise are fully present beings who understand the implications of their actions because they have a sense of the whole right now, in this moment.

Shapeshifting and the web of life: the link for shamans

Shamans in traditional cultures see themselves as integrally connected to the world and to other living and non-living things, all of which they believe are imbued with spirit. That includes things that we typically think of as non-living. Things like rocks, mountains, oceans, and the planet as a whole can be viewed through the shamanic lens as having spirit. Of course James Lovelock's Gaia theory similarly argues that the Earth itself is a living system[66] and some, particularly ecologists, accept that theory. There are even theories that the entire universe is itself conscious,[67] although the form of consciousness differs from the type of self-awareness that we humans typically identify as consciousness.

The perspective that spirit is pervasive is a characteristic of most shamanic traditions, where what is conscious includes humans, of course, but also living beings of all shapes and sizes, from insects to plants to animals. Because this notion is extended to non-living beings as well, such a perspective naturally means that shamans honor the world around them. This honoring is quite different from the ways that many in modern Western cultures, which tend to view mind and body, body and spirit, as separate things, view humans' relationship to the natural world and its other living beings.

We all, I believe, can benefit from this shamanic perspective. We face a troubled world—fraught with climate change, exploitation of natural resources, and overuse of agricultural and other chemicals. We face what some call the sixth great species extinction, during the Holocene epoch, which we are currently moving out of towards what is called the Anthropocene, in which human activities are causing climate change and other dramatic shifts in the world. In this context, we also face increasingly violent weather patterns, drought and desertification in some areas, with violent storms in others, rising temperatures, shrinking glaciers, rising oceans, and numerous other problematic changes in our natural environment.

Today, we face a world with any number of social ills, including growing inequity, intractable poverty, gaps in access to resources and technologies, terrorism, dangerous fundamentalisms of various sorts, huge problems with food and agricultural production and distribution systems, and issues with energy resources. We face massive divisiveness in our political and social systems. Globally, for far too many people there is an enormous crisis around the creation and maintenance of decent livelihoods. In short, these and related problems suggest that we humans have not valued, honored, and respected the world around us sufficiently, despite the fact that it is our only home. In far too many cases, we have similarly not valued other people and certainly not other living beings, not to mention our forests, oceans, plains, mountains, lakes, rivers, and air, nor our cities where so many people live as designed and living creations.

Considering all the problems, there is reason to think that perhaps honoring the world around us in different ways might help to better integrate the ways and mores of humankind with the capacity of the planet to support our own (human) species—as well as other species. What if we, as shamans, treated the world around us as if it and all of its manifestations had *inherent* worth and dignity. Whether we actually believe it or not, if we act "as if" we believe there is spirit in everything and we *treat* these aspects of nature *as if* they have spirit, humans' relationship with the world and with each other, not to mention other living beings, would be vastly more harmonious. What if we treated other species, not to mention other human beings, with respect and dignity even when they were different from ourselves? What if we treated the natural environment with an equal amount of respect and dignity, as if it has inherent worth, not just worth because of what we can exploit for human use? In many respects, that level of respect and dignity is the direction in which a shamanic perspective would lead.

Shamans, particularly today's shamans who think systemically and holistically about their world, understand its complex reality, which is fundamentally supported by up-to-date conceptions from physics of the world as a complex, interconnected web of being.[68] In effect, physicists tell us that the world and indeed the universe is a single, integrated system where what happens in one element influences what is going on throughout the system, sometimes subtly and sometimes more overtly. Physicists, ecologists, biologists, some neurologists, and many other scientists now believe that the world is in fact just such an interconnected web. Further, physicists tell us that every atom within us was present at the origin of the universe and will pass into other things when we die. Such an understanding connects us intimately with all other living and non-living things in the universe. That perspective allows a very different perspective on our relationship with others and to the world around us, placing us as human beings living at a certain point in time in direct relationship to and connection with the world around us—past, present, and future.[69]

What does all of this have to do with shapeshifting? Shapeshifting is the imaginal or mythical ability of the shaman to transform from one type of thing to another. Shamans are frequently said to be shapeshifters, transforming themselves into animals, trees, or other natural entities, even other people at times. Shapeshifting represents a metamorphosis from one type of being to another. Various forms of it are found in mythologies from many different cultures around the world. The idea can be found, for example, in Celtic, Greco-Roman, and Native American folklore, Indian, Philippines, Tatar, Chinese, Japanese, and Korean mythologies, among many others, as well as in a great many works of fiction and fairy tales. The fact that the idea of shapeshifting is so popular suggests the power that such a practice might have in allowing the shaman to "see" (feel, hear, taste, experience, sense in some way) what it is like to *be* some other being or entity. The ability to put yourself into another's shoes is in a sense what shapeshifting is for today's shamans—and that is an activity associated with advanced post-conventional stages of consciousness.

The idea of shapeshifting is ancient and was often associated with gods and goddesses in early mythologies. Shapeshifting can be found in many myths and stories today and, like shamans themselves, in virtually all cultures. Shapeshifting as a transmutation from one form into another is, of course, something we all do when we are conceived, as we grow and mature, and again when we die. In some respects, we are all shapeshifting constantly in the flux and flow of life itself. Thus, in fact, when you think about it, we are constantly shapeshifting throughout our lives physically, moving from being infants to toddlers to children to adolescents to young adults to middle-aged to seniors, and finally to death, which transmutes us into something that is no longer recognizable as our "self." In traditional cultures, shamans are often believed to shapeshift into animals, sometimes into one of the shaman's "power animals," i.e., a helper who can provide insight and wisdom to the shaman. It could be another person, a spirit guide, or it could be some natural entity, like a tree, a rock, or a lake or river.

We also (shape)shift—or develop—across multiple capacities of what Harvard psychologist Howard Gardner calls "intelligences."[70] Particularly relevant among these intelligences to the shaman are intellectual or cognitive, moral, emotional, and spiritual capacities, which continue to evolve and develop over our lifetimes. For example, the way that a child thinks about what is right and wrong is substantially different from the way that an adult thinks about such issues. The adult's thinking is more complex and nuanced than that of the child, encompassing earlier perspectives but moving beyond them. Considerable work by developmental psychologists like Robert Kegan, Bill Torbert, and philosopher Ken Wilber,[71] among others, supports this understanding of human development as growing and developing over the course of the lifespan. It is a form of "shapeshifting" in which we are all engaged whether we recognize it or not.

The type of personality shifting happens through the developmental process just discussed. Societal shapeshifting involves shifts in culture, expectations, mores, and norms or what the biologist Richard Dawkins[72] called "memes," i.e., core cultural artifacts, and which Susan Blackmore has studied extensively.[73] Meme shifts can result from multiple dynamics, including changing understanding, creating new stories and narratives, developing new ideas and images, technological shifts, changing norms and behaviors, media influences, artistic creations, and any number of other factors, often promulgated by shamanic individuals who in their own way do the healing, connecting, and sensemaking work of the shaman.

The author John Perkins, who has written extensively about shamanism, explicitly discusses three levels of shapeshifting—cellular, personality, and societal transformation—in a book called *Shapeshifting*.[74] Statements of cellular-level shapeshifting, i.e., the actual transformation of the shaman into, say, a jaguar, or other forms of transmutation, which Perkins claims to have witnessed, may deserve investigation. The general idea that shamans can, by journeying into other realms, experience for example what it is like to be a tree or a jaguar imaginally (that is, realistically in the imagination), is more plausible to the Western mind.

The idea of the imaginal is important here because imaginal realms are very "real," in that they can be quite vividly experienced. Indeed, most belief systems, cultural artifacts, and sets of accepted "ways we do things here," as examples, are imaginal in the sense that they encompass a degree of realism or strong set of beliefs that go beyond simple imagination. Such imaginal images are quite genuine and can powerfully shape perspectives on the world. The memes[75] on which we base our worldviews, cultural stories and narratives, and belief systems, which are fundamentally ideas, have similar imaginal qualities of realism.

Shapeshifting is at its core an imaginal experience, the attempt to "become" something different and to see through the lens of that something, allowing us to broaden our perspectives and learn to respect the thing that we are experiencing imaginally.

Because of their ability to imaginally shapeshift, traditional shamans tend not see themselves as separate from other creatures and entities in the world. Indeed, the shamanic notion of shapeshifting suggests that shamans can transmute into other things—a tree, for instance—because, in effect, they already *are* these things because of our integral interconnectedness with what physicist Fritjof Capra calls the "web of life,"[76] a web that intricately and intimately links everything in existence. Today's shamans can reach a similar state without the use of mind-altering concoctions or extreme experiences, through various meditative and mindfulness practices that focus attention and allow the imagination to soar. Simply sitting quietly and allowing the mind to focus on the question of what it would be like to be, e.g., a tree, a lake, or an animal that attracts you, can be a powerful experience that takes you out of your current context and allows you to gain insight into that other entity's existence.

Whether a shaman or physicist, ecologist, or simply someone who can see this interconnectedness, in doing this your worldview shifts. If you believe yourself connected to everything else in our world, if you believe that all things are interdependent, and if you recognize that there is a chain of interlinked subatomic particles, atoms, molecules, and bigger constructions going from the Big Bang to ourselves, that perspective can have a profound effect on your relationship with the world around you. Those things we are integrally connected to, we honor in ways that we might not do if we felt somehow separated or disconnected. That honoring of the world around us and others who might or might not be like us, and helping others to do so as well, is part of today's shaman's work.

In a sense, as human beings, we frequently shapeshift: for instance, by changing our minds, and developing new roles, skills, and talents. For example, when we set a new goal for ourselves and work hard to attain new capabilities that will help us achieve that goal, there is a sense in which we are shapeshifting. You might be working, say, in business, and decide that your true calling is to become a nurse. In going to nursing school, you are transforming yourself in significant ways— acquiring new knowledge and insights, learning new skills, and taking on the values and attitudes associated with nursing. Similar transformations happen to all of us when we make educational choices, career shifts, engage in passionate pursuits, go on a diet or start exercising (and quite literally reshape our bodies sometimes), and otherwise set goals that we work hard to achieve. So, for example, you might decide to become a musician, dancer, or artist as a hobby, and this new activity changes and reshapes the way you think about yourself and how you act in the world.

This type of shapeshifting seems quite "normal," i.e., taking place in everyday reality. We are all familiar with these shifts of shape. Though we do not necessarily call the process shapeshifting, such transformations require us to go outside of our usual boundaries and enter into new experiences that change and shape us in new ways. When we engage with such experiences fully and truly enter into the new pursuit, whatever it might be, we do change who we are and how we interact with the world and those others around us, sometimes subtly and sometimes more obviously as we integrate these shifts into our beings.

The practice of shapeshifting shamanically asks us to deliberately and with intention step into the "being" and power of
another living being or entity. Good actors do this constantly—
"becoming" in a sense the person they are portraying. Can you
"become" a mountain, e.g., in yoga practice, for example, by
being still and using your imagination to try to experience what
the mountain must experience. Could you open up in meditation or the tree pose in yoga to what a tree might experience
under differing circumstances? Can you sing a song and allow
yourself to "become" the song? Can you attempt imaginally to
"see" through the eyes of another person—maybe someone you
love or perhaps someone with whom you are disagreeing—to
attempt to figure out why they do and say what they do?

All of these experiences use your shamanic power of stepping
into non-ordinary reality to begin to experience something new
and quite different than what you experience every day, and
enhance your shapeshifting abilities. Think how you can begin
to shift your perspective on the world around us if you imaginally "become" a tree or river damaged by pollution and attempt
to see the world from that entity's perspective.

Shapeshifting is powerful because it helps you find empathy
and resonance with others. Being able to do such perspective-
taking work is important in many healing processes because it
enhances understanding and the ability to know what needs to
shift. Shapeshifting can also be a powerful way for you to transform yourself so that you can reach your goals or master some
new skill. Alcoholics Anonymous asks its participants, for
example, to act "as if" they have already achieved control over
their disease. This "as if" acting is a powerful act of shapeshifting. If you want to achieve in your career, you can apply shapeshifting similarly by acting "as if" you are already advanced in

your career. For example, by dressing appropriately for the position you want, acquiring the necessary skills and education, seeking input and advice from others who have already mastered what you are aiming for and acting more like they act, you are performing an act of shapeshifting. If you want to be happier, one way of doing that is to act "as if" you are happier, place yourself in the company of others who are content or happy with their situations, because emotions are contagious and readily transferred from one person to another. The "as if" you are happy helps, because, for example, when you smile, your brain cannot tell that it is an "as if" you are happy smile from a real one—and you start to feel better.

Be careful when attempting to shapeshift, though, especially if you are shapeshifting to powerful creatures or entities. It is always important to respect the "being" of the other entities into which we are shapeshifting, because some of their power transfers to us as we "become" them imaginally. This respect is necessary for you to use the power that you gain through shapeshifting in positive ways, i.e., as the shaman does for healing, connecting, and sensemaking purposes that serve the world. In traditional ceremonies of shapeshifting, shamans always show gratitude (and sometimes give small gifts like salt or herbs) to the being whose shape they have taken as a measure of respect, because the shaman fundamentally believes that there is spirit in everything, which, as we will see below, can be an important element in transforming our world for the better—the central role of today's shaman.

Fear, love, and the shaman

My teacher John Myerson says that we can live in one of two states: fear or love. Much of the public conversation in the United States and elsewhere these days seems to come from a place of fear. Fear fuels the election of politicians who are corrupt, abusive bullies (or worse), the epidemic of gun violence, the rage and hatred of people who are unlike ourselves, and many other social ills. But fear and its manifestations in action cannot solve these problems.

Part of the healing task of the shaman is to help people live in and come from a place of love in their lives rather than a place of fear. "Love" in this usage is the opposite of fear. It implies an expansiveness, an open awareness, an ability to work towards positive ends, to collaborate as well as compete, to work generatively towards the health and wellbeing of the whole at whatever level we work best at. One way today's shamans in a variety of fields can do this is by helping others learn how to face or "walk through" their fear. Doing this can help to convert unreasonable or unrealistic fears into manageable situations that can help avoid many problems and engender a much more healthy attitude towards life and its numerous situations.

Fear creates stress, which is both physically and emotionally damaging. Fear develops when we feel threatened in some way. Maybe there is real danger and the fear response is both reasonable and useful because it enables to get out of the way of the danger. In many situations, however, fear is triggered by old patterns and responses to situations that we only *perceive* to be dangerous or threatening, but that really will not do us any physical, psychic, or emotional harm.

Fear can be overwhelming and cause us to freeze, a kind of paralysis, so that we are unable to act in the situation. Fear can trigger the "fight or flight" response, causing us to escalate a situation that otherwise need not be escalated. We have seen this type of escalation too often in reports of police interactions with people they have arrested or stopped for minor causes, hate crimes, and the election of abusive and regressive politicians, who look like they will play "good father"[77] to the populace despite their bullying ways. The "flight" response might be simply to run away and hide your head in the sand, which can sometimes work for a time. Too often, though, flight responses create even more problems because the fear still exists and reactions can be triggered in the person (or entity) that one fears, including ill health, relationship problems, and, at a larger level, societal problems when major issues are ignored. Think of running away from the police as an example—it typically creates more problems than it helps.

Fear can take many forms, including fear of death or harm, even fear that someone will outperform you in some way: i.e., fear of losing. Some people fear insects, snakes, or other creatures. Others fear people unlike themselves, finding it hard to have compassion for or understanding of people who are different. Still other fears involve the unknown or the new: i.e., a fear of change. As adults, we have typically had many experiences with the potential to induce fear, because results of past experiences have not always been positive. So we face similar situations with fear rather than love, hope, or more importantly action aimed at a better outcome. All of these situations result in stress, especially if the fear is maintained over long periods of time.

The stress caused by fear can have emotional, physiological, behavioral, and mental consequences. Among the physical consequences are muscle tension or pain, headaches, chest pains, and problems sleeping. Emotional consequences can include anxiety, restlessness, problems motivating yourself, feeling overwhelmed, sadness and depression, and sometimes anger or irritation. Stress can cause us to over-eat, abuse drugs, alcohol, or tobacco, and even withdraw from social activities. Further, stress has been associated with a number of health problems, especially when it is prolonged.

All of the causes of stress and fears need to be carefully evaluated as to whether there is a realistic potential for harm. If real harm is likely, then fight, flight, avoidance, or dealing effectively with the source of fear, including new actions and behaviors, may well be needed. But many of our fears and related stresses are irrational and even subconscious, based on negative past experiences. Here is where the work of the shaman can become helpful in leading us through the fear to face the source of fear, and question whether it is being helpful—or getting in our way of being more effective in life, at work, or in doing whatever it is we wish to do.

Fear can hold us back from becoming fully who we are. For example, we may underachieve or enter into activities that do not really appeal to us because we are afraid of disappointing others by not meeting their expectations. Sometimes we are afraid of disappointing ourselves. Think, for example, of the expectations that your parents may have had for your work, marriage, or other important aspects of life—and whether or not those expectations are congruent with your own desire. Have you ever chosen to do something or act in a certain way to meet the expectations of others, even when you know deep inside yourself that is somehow "not you"? Have you ever let fear, e.g., of failure or not meeting others' expectations, hold you back from pursuing a much-desired goal? Do you really fear that someone will break into your home to terrorize you so much that you need an arsenal of guns? Or that your neighbor, who may look different from you, has your worst interests at heart? Have you even tried getting to know those neighbors to find out whether your fears are justified?

Think of the things you fear. Maybe it's failing at something you hoped to accomplish. Maybe it's the fear of never being loved or of being abandoned by someone you love. Maybe it's the fear of facing your own weaknesses . . . or having others find out about them. Maybe it's even the fear of being successful. For as Marianne Williamson, who was quoted by Nelson Mandela, once said in her own shamanic wisdom:

> Our deepest fear is not that we are inadequate. Our deep-est fear is that we are powerful beyond measure. It is our light, not our darkness, that most frightens us. We ask our-selves, Who am I to be brilliant, gorgeous, talented, and fabulous?[78]

The interesting thing is that Williamson continues by asking us, as shamanic practice does, to walk through our fears to find out what is on the other side of them:

> Actually, who are you *not* to be? You are a child of God [the universe]. Your playing small does not serve the world. There is nothing enlightened about shrinking so that other people will not feel insecure around you. We are all meant to shine, as children do. . . . As we are liberated from our own fear, our presence automatically liberates others.[79]

The shaman works from a place of healing, love, and har-mony with the universe, rather than from a place of fear. Because shamans have to first heal themselves, they have gone through their own fears and understand how powerful these fears can be. They deal with new fears or the reappearance of old ones as they arise—for they inevitably will. The shamanic healer (perhaps a good therapist, or even yourself if you can gain insight into the fear on your own) can help you face and understand the nature of whatever fear is holding you back, or the reality of the fears that might be making you lash out at others or make unwise choices.

You can then call up in your imagination (imaginally) what you believe to be the source of that fear and talk to it as a player in your psyche/spirit who is holding you back. You can put yourself in the role of the grown and loving person you are today in the conversation and send love to the you that was getting the messages that are now holding you back. You can let that part of you that is holding you back know that it no longer needs to be held back by those messages and old stories. Then you can see if, with the help of your own shamanic powers or the powers of another healer and some of this hard work, you can actually walk through the fear(s) to find out what the possibilities are on the other side of them so that you can begin to act from a place of love.

6

Science, the shaman, and our world

Fundamentally, I am a skeptic about many things, even or especially many things associated with shamanism. I don't think we can ever know for certain whether shamanic practice "works" or not, because what it exactly is and how it works is mysterious. When we are working shamanically, by definition, we are operating in non-ordinary reality—using instincts, intuitions, insights, creative impulses, and the like. Such experiences are achieved through a variety of practices to access knowledge, information, and insights, not necessarily through analytical, deductive, or otherwise rational or logical ways of thinking and operating. Thus, this skepticism remains true despite having studied shamanic practice in today's context with a group for years, having read widely in and about shamanism, and having even attempted to practice it.

Trained as a social scientist in organizational behavior and management, I have for years studied corporate responsibility, collaboration, difference making, and most recently intellectual shamanism in management academics, among other topics. My bent, therefore, is thinking about the ways shamanic practice, however conceived, might be practiced in today's distressed world. This thinking naturally moves towards thinking about how shamans could help heal businesses, economies, and societies and their troubled relationships with each other and the natural world. To begin, let's briefly consider what science might be able to tell us about shamanic practice today.

Shamanism, science, and skepticism

One can accomplish studies of just about anything from an empirically based, positivist stance. Most scientists operate in the context of disciplines, just as most academics and scholars do. Although there has been a move in recent years for so-called hard sciences, i.e., the ones that use empirical measures, to integrate across scientific disciplines using multiple and multi-disciplinary co-researchers on studies, there still exists a positivist bias in much science. Positivism, as a scientific approach, means that scientific assertions need to be justified rationally, logically, through mathematical proofs, or empirical results drawn from natural phenomena.

This positivist approach has infected much of social science as well, leaving the impression that all or the only valid knowledge is that drawn from empirical, mathematical, or logical deduction. With these beliefs, societies, communities, organizations, and people are also supposed to behave according to general laws, rationalistic and empirically based understandings, and scientific evidence. From the positivist perspective, intuitive or introspective knowledge, insights, and understanding are often dismissed as simply being metaphysics, irrationally, or unverifiable. Shamanism, from this perspective, which still pervades much of Western thought, is considered irrational or mysterious—and not worth much attention.

There are alternative approaches, however, that value the insights that come from introspection, meditation, reflection, and non-observable resources that are traditionally tapped by the shaman. Polymath and philosopher Ken Wilber has developed his integral framework to develop a holistic conception of living systems.[80] Wilber in numerous books (without arguing for shamanism explicitly) claims that, to understand anything fully, you need to understand it through four lenses: objective/individual, objective/collective, subjective/individual, and subjective/collective. These four lenses cover the empirically based and logical/rational approaches of science in the objective quadrants. They also make room for the interior, more subjectively, and experientially derived understandings that come from internal or subjective ways of understanding the world. The key, for Wilber, is that a complete understanding requires not just one perspective, but all four. The problem posed by positivists is that they are typically coming from the perspective of only one (objectively based) lens.

An example may help. In understanding "understanding," as an example, the objective/individual perspective looks at, e.g., a single human brain and how it functions neurologically and in other empirically observable and measurable ways. An objective/collective perspective might, for example, compare measurements of individual brain functioning across a number of individuals or some group of individuals to see how they are similar and different. A subjective/individual perspective might, for example, be associated with psychological understandings of how the brain functions from the perspective of the person having a variety of experiences, which, as Wilber notes, we can only "know" by asking that individual. Finally, an objective/collective perspective might consider group behaviors and practices or culture to understand how brains function, which can only be known experientially either by asking members of the group or participating in the group and carefully observing what is going on.

Wilber's most important point with his integral framework is that, to understand anything fully, you really need to understand it not from just one of these perspectives but from *all four* perspectives. The scientific perspective, whether at the individual or collective level of analysis, typically uses only one of these perspectives—and that is where the integral or more holistic perspective of the shaman becomes relevant. Many scientists (and management academics) would like to believe that they can be and are "objective" in their observations. If Wilber is correct that we need to understand all four perspectives, then viewing a phenomenon from just one perspective, as most disciplines tend to do, is limiting and cannot conceivably provide an integrated—holistic—understanding.

Over years of doing management research and scholarship, I have come to realize that, really, there is little that we can actually term "objective." Simply choosing to focus on a particular question, issue, or problem creates a context that shapes what is likely to be found or discovered in any kind of study, as well as how you approach it, and what question(s) get asked. Thus, we can look at any issues through eyes that recognize all four "quadrants" of Wilber's integral framework. How we choose to look at a problem or issue is a subjective decision, although we may not always be aware of this decision. This lack of "objectivity" becomes particularly clear when complex systems or what are called "wicked" problems are involved. With wicked problems there is difficulty in determining where problems begin and end, where different stakeholders bring different points of view to the problem definition, and to how an issue can be determined to have been successfully resolved. And most human systems and living beings are complex systems—or are interacting continually with complex systems.[81]

At the same time, it is important to recognize that there are measurable and observable things in the world, things we typically term "objective." Shamans in our world deal with both the subjective and inter-subjective aspects of the situations they are working on—and, equally importantly, the more measurable and observable elements: the so-called objective elements. Thus, the choice of research method, approach, particular data to look at, and how one approaches all of these questions, including the framing of the research question itself, all shape the outcome of any study, as well as what can be learned from it—and these things also shape the work of the shaman in all arenas.

Skepticism remains. Skepticism in this context simply means maintaining a questioning attitude, or suspending judgment. I believe that such skepticism is a healthy attitude, even towards empirical evidence (which can sometimes be manipulated). Unless I experience something myself and can somehow "test" it (not always possible), it seems best to remain skeptical. But skepticism, though helpful in our science-based world, seems unhelpful at best when it comes to shamanic powers and interventions. What can I say but that trust—trusting what I call the universe (others may use words to signify a higher power of some sort)—is important. There have been many times when I have experienced such synchronicity—or things happening as I had desired—which lead me to believe there is some element of shamanic power at work in them.

Shamans, physics, and Schrödinger's cat

Shamanism, to many Western minds, is quite strange, weird— or *wyrd* in the mystical sense. Shamans are thought to retrieve information from some deep source (the "universe," Spirit, or collective unconscious) and use it for healing purposes. The exact mechanisms for doing this, to the extent that it is effective, are not well understood—and vary widely across cultures. Shamans use and tap into energy in different ways to gather needed information and then use it for healing purposes.

Despite wide cultural differences, there seems to be some sort of universality to the ways of the shaman. The differences also pointedly indicate that there is no one "right" way to be a shaman. Here I have argued for a path to shamanic practice that taps into today's sensibilities and understandings without the magico-religious trappings that underpin many traditional shamanic practices. That is particularly important, I think, for shamans today, who operate within the context of a dominant scientific (and economic) (rather than mystical, mythological, or religious) paradigm.

In other words, I am trying to understand (and convey that understanding of) shamanism as a potentially powerful way for people operating within today's context to operate as healers, connectors, and sensemakers in serving the world and the common good. Many people arguably do the work of shamanism without necessarily resorting to practices that are common and acceptable in traditional cultures but which seem somehow out of place or strange in many modern settings.

Perhaps some additional reflections on emerging understandings in physics can place shamanism into today's context. Physics now tells us that, at the quantum level, the universe we live is far more mysterious than once believed. Indeed, to date, quantum physics remains a mystery even to physicists, never mind the rest of us. Set in the context of modern physics, the weirdness and almost mystical qualities associated with shamanic practice somehow seem less daunting. The fact that physics tells us that, at the most fundamental or quantum level, our universe itself is very strange and, to date at least, somewhat incomprehensible, at least provides an opportunity to explore shamanism's "strangeness" with a more open perspective, since, today, most of us trust scientists to be seeking and hopefully finding "truth," whatever that might be.

This strangeness in physics is exemplified in what has become known as the "Schrödinger's cat" thought experiment (also called the observer effect), designed by physicist Erwin Schrödinger. A cat is placed into a box, along with a toxic radioactive substance, of which, in the course of an hour, an atom may or may not have decayed—both events having equal probability in that time. After an hour had elapsed, the cat is said to be either dead or alive. There is no way of knowing until the box is opened, so, theoretically, the cat remains in suspension between life and death until that time of being observed. Schrödinger meant this thought experiment to explain the paradoxes and uncertainty inherent in quantum physics.

I would note that the Schrödinger's cat thought experiment reminds me of a similar one told by my New Zealand friend and colleague Edwina Pio about a Zen master:

There is a story of two disciples who wished to test the
Zen master to see if he really knew all that people said he
was supposed to know. Their plan was the following: They
caught a small bird that fitted in the palm of their hand.
They decided that they would keep the bird in the closed
palm of their hand and ask the master if the bird was dead
or alive. If the master said it was alive, they would crush
the bird in their hand and then open their hand to show it
was dead. If the master said it was dead, they would open
their palm and let the bird fly away. With this strategy in
mind, they went to visit the master while he was giving a
public discourse. They raised their hands and said they had
a question. "Go ahead" said the master. Then they posed
their question: "Master, master, with your great knowledge, please can you tell us if the bird in our hand is dead
or alive?" The master looked at them, smiled, and said,
"Hope is in your hands."[82]

To what extent does hope play out in the work of the shaman,
whose sensemaking gifts help provide hope and healing through
new understandings and through the body's and the world's
capacity to heal itself when given the right motivation?

Let us continue to explore physics a little more to further
comprehend some of its strangeness today as it relates to shamanic practice. In addition to the cat thought experiment, at the
quantum level physicists long debated whether light is a particle
or a wave. It turns out that, depending on how you measure it,
it is both, even though those states seem to be contradictory or
paradoxical. The analogy that I make here is that, as with the
cat in the box so with the duality of light, we cannot really
know with certainty how or whether shamanic interventions
work or are mere coincidences until we look into the box. Even
then, our "knowing" depends, as does much science, according
to the Heisenberg uncertainty principle and modern understand-

ings of atomic particles, on what we look at and how we choose to do the looking.[83]

In another strange aspect of modern physics, Heisenberg's uncertainty principle says that, for quantum particles, we can never really know precisely those properties that are linked to each other. That is, the position and momentum, or speed, of a quantum particle are tied together in a way that says that the more precisely one of these attributes is measured, the less precisely the other can be determined. The state of an atomic particle in an atom cannot be determined in advance of its measurement because the act of measuring determines the outcome. Atomic states are, essentially, probabilistic in that they have a *probability* of being a certain state but that state cannot be known for sure until it is measured. Thus, a light particle is either a wave or a particle depending on how it is measured. Before it is measured it exists simultaneously in both states—as potential.

Further, and perhaps even stranger, at the quantum level, if an atom is what is called "entangled" with another atom or deeply connected, they in a sense act as a unit. If the state of one atom changes (i.e., shifts position, momentum, spin, or polarization), the state of the other instantaneously changes. This shift happens no matter how far apart the particles are.

The other thing that modern physics tells us is that everything is, at core, energy, and that all energy is dynamically interrelated, interdependent, and connected. The world and indeed the universe is constantly in flux, both at the quantum and very macro levels, as well as at our middle level of understanding. We are all deeply connected to the universe since we are all formed out of the great explosion called the "Big Bang" that brought our universe into existence. Everything we can experience today was present at the time of the Big Bang, perhaps in different form. Thus, we are all, as Joni Mitchell sang years ago, in a very real sense, made of stardust,[84] in that every atom in our being was part of that initial Big Bang. So we as humans (as well as everything else in our world) are deeply interconnected with our very beginnings and with everything else in the universe.

Psychologist Carl Jung posited, as noted earlier, something like a collective unconscious, which I have argued is what shamans tap into in journeying, reflective, and ritualistic practices. Perhaps, then, it is that deep connection to the energies of the past, present, or perhaps future that shamans connect with when they journey or when in various other states of trance seek information and knowledge. Since we are all comprised of what has always existed in our universe, then perhaps there are ways, through altered states of consciousness or otherwise, to access this knowledge. Whatever it is, shamans understand these deep interrelationships, energies, and connections. It is an essential part of the work of the shaman to help others understand such relationships, energies, and connections as well.

What does all of this science, particularly physics, have to do with shamanism? Well, here is my speculation—and that is all it is. At core, everything we know and experience is energy. Shamans work with energy. To the extent that shamans heal themselves, they are changing their own energy. If everything is interconnected and dynamically related as physics today argues, then changing your own energy to be more healed, more positive, brings about more positive energy in the world. Similarly, if shamans gather information through the use of their powers and use that information for positive purposes, for healing patients, communities, or the world around them, then they are changing that energy as well—and that has positive ramifications, possibly even instantaneously, spreading throughout the universe. If this speculation is correct, and of course from more my skeptical, scientific perspective, that is a big "if," then if many more people engage in shifting their own and others' energies in positive and constructive (for the world) directions, then significant change can begin to happen. We continue to explore these ideas below.

Mystical thinking and the shaman

In biological systems, new understanding about how genes work suggests that genes and environment interact to create the characteristics of an individual—not that the gene alone determines what those characteristics will be. This new biological approach is called epigenetics.[85] Similarly, scientists of consciousness now understand consciousness to be both an emergent process that is highly non-linear and not "material" in the "stuff" sense of the word, and necessarily subjective.

For many years, scientists believed (and many still do!) that physical matter and mind processes could be separated and distinguished. There was (and is, for some) a split between mind and matter that is often called the "Cartesian split," because it derives from philosopher René Descartes' notion that "I think, therefore I am." The result of this thinking is a belief that there is a necessary distinction between mind and body. Of course, this belief in Western civilization has extended to a belief that "man" is separate from nature, a belief that from a scientific perspective is patently false, since humans are integrally and inextricably linked to and part of nature. The emergence of complexity science in the late 20th and into the 21st century, combined with the contributions of quantum physics, demonstrate quite powerfully that such distinctions are not the way that the world—or consciousness—actually works.

Physicist Fritjof Capra and co-author Pier Luigi Luisi comment on the empirical nature of both physics experiments and meditative insights. The former derives from observation of physical phenomena, the latter from what can be seen in consciousness, meditatively, by looking within and being experienced by the individual. Capra and Luisi state:

> The mystic looks within and explores his consciousness at various levels, including the physical phenomena associated with the mind's embodiment. The physicist, by contrast, begins his inquiry into the essential nature of things by studying the material world. Exploring ever deeper realms of matter, he becomes aware of the essential unity of all natural phenomena. More than that, he also realizes that he himself and his consciousness are an integral part of this unity. Thus the mystic and the physicist arrive at the same conclusion; one starting from the inner realm, and the other from the outer world. The harmony between their views confirms the ancient Indian wisdom that *brahman*, the ultimate reality without, is identical to *atman*, the reality within.[86]

In the trance state, the shaman is said to access other, typically spiritual, realms to gather information needed to heal patients or communities. Modern shamans too cross boundaries or barriers that many others do not cross, because they tend to think holistically and recognize the need for information from a variety of sources to begin to gain understanding of a system, situation, or set of ideas. Shamans' holistic thinking is integrative in its nature, drawing from both subjective and objective phenomena at the individual and collective levels, much as what needs to be done to fully understand something, according to Ken Wilber's integral framework.[87]

Consciousness, it seems, emerges and shifts over time and throughout adult life as people go through various developmental stages, becoming broader and more encompassing with such development. For example, a lot of cognitive and moral development theory suggests that, early on, the individual's worldview is quite limited—to the self, and ultimately to a few others, as in the family. As the person matures, the reference group becomes social (think teenagers referring to their friends as the most important arbiter of what's important in life), and then begins to encompass the tribe, community, or society. This stage is called conventional development. Post-conventional development, which not everyone achieves according to empirical research,[88] involves understanding that there are multiple systems and multiple perspectives, each with their own set of rules, values, and norms—which are different but that one is not necessarily better than others. Wilber tracks further developmental stages associated with mystics and other transcendent persons, such as some shamans, who tap into other worlds or realms, or what I have called the universe, to gain understanding.

Wilber, who has studied and integrated a wide variety of developmental theories, notes that human beings experience differing states, stages, and structures of consciousness.[89] These different states and stages matter when it comes to becoming a shaman. Since the primary goal of the shaman is healing, and since one of the things that shamans do is cross (spiritual and other) boundaries to gather information needed for their connector and sensemaker roles to help in the healing process, the broader a perspective the shaman in the modern world has, arguably the better.

States or state-stages are the ways in which individuals experience the world directly from what Wilber calls the "first person" or subjective perspective. There are numerous systems and labels that explain the various states of consciousness. Wilber synthesizes these states into: waking, dreaming, deep formless sleep, Witnessing (also called unqualifiable Awareness), and non-dual awakened "Suchness." Sometimes the latter two are combined, leaving four major states that are aligned with body (or the gross physical realm), mind (or the subtle mind realm), soul (or the causal Witnessing or Real Self realm), and spirit (or the non-dual "Suchness" or "Unity" realm). The most fully developed and "awakened" or aware state is spirit or non-duality, a state in which one sees the oneness of all being, according to Wilber.

States or state-stages can be fluid and are not necessarily permanent; they, in a sense, depend on what the person is doing and where the focus is at a given time, though certain practices like meditation, shamanic journeying, introspection, reflection, and visioning, for example, can enhance the possibility of staying in a more advanced state-stage for longer periods of time. Over time and with appropriate developmental activities, there is progression in the state-stages, moving from body to mind to soul to spirit in a loose way, with the idea that the higher-order stages will become more permanent as they are more experienced.

Structure stages of consciousness, according to Wilber, are the mental models, patterns, or mindsets, effectively worldviews, through which people perceive the world around them. Structure stages emerge in a definitive order and cannot be skipped (unlike state-stages, in which higher states can sometimes be experienced for a short period of time and then the individual goes back to the main state-stage that she or he is at). When a new developmental level is achieved, the individual leaves behind the previous structure or worldview for a broader, more encompassing worldview or structure-stage. The old structure or worldview is subsumed under the bigger umbrella of the newer one, still existing, but no longer dominant so the person is able to see the world through what amounts to a broader lens. One set of labels (out of many possible labels, depending on the author or system in use) for these worldviews starting from the lowest level, called archaic, moves to magic, mythic, rational, pluralistic, integral, and super-integral.

The analogy that Wilber makes about the changing worldview is that of climbing a ladder. As you scale each rung, your perspective shifts and you identify that the new perspective, recognize that the old structure is still there, but, in effect, have transcended and encompassed that old perspective with the new structure or worldview. These state-stages and structure-stages are consistent across geographical regions and cultures, because they are part of the way in which the brain/body itself develops.

Awareness can be developed by a variety of techniques including, most importantly, meditation and mindfulness techniques, but also introspection, visioning, and shamanic journeying, among others. In fact, one of the prescriptions for moving from one state to another is to engage in some form of meditative or mindfulness practice. Many traditional shamans are in what Wilber,[90] following Graves[91] and other developmental theorists call magic, mythic, egocentric, or absolutist stages of development. Today, the crises of our times call for many more of us in general, and particularly those of us who would act as shaman healers, to move beyond these stages towards broader, more complexly nested, and comprehensive stages of development so that we can avoid being, as psychologist Robert Kegan calls it, "in over our heads."[92]

Developmental theorists and physicists thus point out that many types of exploration and observation take place in realms that are inaccessible to others by ordinary means. Journeying and various ways of reaching trance or other forms of meditative and hypnotic states are helpful in moving individuals along this developmental path. As noted earlier, they are important practices that many, though not all, shamans engage in. Today's shaman needs to evolve to the highest possible level, i.e., structure-stage and consistent state-stage, so that she or he can deal with the manifold problems and complexity of the world holistically, realistically, and with compassion and understanding. Shamans need to be able to bring all their resources to dealing with relationships of all sorts in our troubled world.

Such is also true of the insights that the traditional shaman brings from his or her journeys to spiritual realms, for they most resemble the insights gained from various types of reflective practices. Making connections across the realms of everyday reality is less problematic, and today's shamans often make such links that others have not yet made through the connecting function. By crossing boundaries or bridging areas that other do not typically cross, today's shamans can "see" what is not usually seen by others and therefore is not immediately accessible to others, at least until the shaman makes sense of it. This "seeing" is not "ordinary," because not everyone is willing to or capable of doing it, just as not everyone is willing to engage in meditative and reflective practices that open up inner resources.

We can call the skill to see across boundaries or make bridges across systems and ideas mystical. Or we can recognize this ability simply as a more holistic way of viewing the world that can be gained through a variety of practices and insights, drawing from all four of Wilber's quadrants. Learning to think and see holistically is, in my view, one of the gifts of the shaman—and something that we can learn if we put our minds (and hearts) to it.

The shaman as an integrative, holistic thinker readily uses experiences gathered from connecting with "other realms" as part of the healing and sensemaking processes. The connecting function involves finding and using new sources of information, ideas and intuitions, and putting those ideas together in new and insightful ways. That is, shamans seek out and "see" (feel, intuit, sense in some way) the ways in which ideas, people, concepts, information from a variety of places can be connected.

There are multiple ways in which consciousness has been studied over the years,[93] ranging from a reductionist (everything reduces to physiology) to a functionalist (behavioral) to neurophenomenology.[94] Neurophenomenology, which derives from the field of phenomenology or the study of experience, integrates direct experience (subjective or "first person" experiences) with exploration of how complex neural patterns and activities are related to those experiences. Thus, consciousness is the interaction of two interdependent things—direct, subjective experience combined with physiological patterns and pathways evidence, e.g., in the firing of neurons that are of interest to reductionist and functionalist perspectives. Scientists interested in the subjective experiences of individuals approach this study in a variety of ways, e.g., phenomenologically by seeking to understand experiences such as perceptions and emotions, which are always "about" something; through introspection and reflection; and through evidence from meditative practices from a range of spiritual and philosophical practices.

Paradox and the shaman

Just as light is both a wave and a particle, depending on how we measure and look at it, the shaman is of one world and of other worlds. In the role of connector, the shaman crosses boundaries to gain new information, and sometimes that information contradicts what is "known" in the original "world." A paradox is a something that seems to lack logic or is self-contradictory. Paradoxes can be found in seeming absurd or contradictory statements, experiences, or situations. Paradoxes are filled with seeming incongruity or inconsistency . . . yet they can be very fruitful ways of seeing the world, since in many apparent paradoxes both of the seemingly opposing positions, experiences, or statements seem to be true.

Shamans can often "hold" paradoxes without worrying about the apparent contradictions in them, sometimes even seeing that there is truth in both perspectives, depending on your point of view. Some artists, like M.C. Escher, are masters of dealing with paradoxes. Consider Escher's famous drawing of hands drawing each other.[95] Realistic-looking hands fade into sketches in which each hand holds a pencil that seems to be drawing the other hand. Where does one start and the other end? How can we understand a paradoxical image like this one? Many of Escher's images illustrate paradoxes. They might feature stairs that go upside down or seemingly in circles[96] or stairs that seem to go on endlessly.[97]

Such images reflect the ability to "hold" the paradox as part of a tension of opposites that often exists in life, where two opposite things are juxtaposed against each other: contradictory, yet simultaneously existing. The shaman, as artist and like the artist, knows that paradoxes can challenge us to think or "see" the world around us in new ways.

Sometimes physical structures can be paradoxical, like, for instance, the Möbius loop. Möbius loops are shapes in which there is only one side and only one boundary? How can this be? In ordinary reality, loops have two sides, but because the two ends are joined after the loop has been twisted, the Möbius loop has only one side. (If you doubt this, create such a loop by taking a narrow strip of paper, half twisting it, and gluing it together as a loop. Then trace its sides and boundaries and you will find there is only one of each, although there are quite obviously two sides when you just look at one piece of the loop.)

Another paradox is exhibited in the old riddle, "Which came first, the chicken or the egg?" There is no obvious answer to this riddle because each seemingly needs to have existed for the other to exist. Such questions take us out of our comfort zones, asking us to consider deeper questions of meaning and how life itself evolved, what the nature of birth is, and, even more importantly, whether there can truly be a traceable initial cause or condition to any given event, especially in the context of complex and dynamic systems—which human and ecological systems inevitably are.

Other paradoxes come from apparent logical flaws. Statements like "I always lie," known as the liar's paradox, are common paradoxes in everyday language. If this statement is accurate, it is—paradoxically—a lie. If it is false, then it is true, which makes the statement false. The key is that both statements can be true statements, but presumably not at the same time. Such paradoxes makes us think, and thinking can lead to changed perspectives and, ultimately, changing, and hopefully healing, our view of the world as we gain broader, more integrated, and complex perspectives, which are part of the human development process in maturity.

Here is where the shaman comes in. Many great healers and teachers understand the power of paradox in healing, particularly healing the mind and the way we perceive the world. Consider the Buddha, a great shaman and healer, and Buddhist philosophy, which often focuses the student of Buddhism on what are known as kōans. Kōans are paradoxical stories or questions that students of Buddhism struggle over. A famous kōan is "What is the sound of one hand clapping?" This apparently paradoxical question or a story or statement forces students of Buddhism to attempt to unpack meaning that the rational mind struggles with. Kōans are meant in Buddhist practice to exhaust rational and thinking responses, fostering great intuitive responses—and thereby enhancing understanding.

The very idea of spiritual realms, often accessed through mindfulness techniques or trance, seems mysterious and somewhat paradoxical to our ordinary-world (and Western) eyes. For many, the material—what we call the real world—is all that seems real to us. Shamans understand that there is more to the world than we can see in the material world, and that sometimes intuition, of the sort that Buddhist kōans are meant to foster, can be helpful as we seek new ideas, innovations, and insights that can bring healing to the world around us.

Shamans' holistic perspective implicitly understands that what we can observe directly is not necessarily all that is. Shamans understand both the rational and the intuitive, the directly observable and the experienced, and attempt to integrate all. Shamans use rational analysis *and* intuition, along intensive study and deep knowledge that can only be experienced directly, for healing purposes. Sometimes shamans "know" intuitively what needs to be done for healing purposes, because somehow they have integrated these four realms, as outlined by Wilber and discussed above. They are then willing to trust that knowledge gathered in unusual ways (e.g., in trance states or by crossing boundaries in a variety of ways) may have validity.

Since the world is a whole, shamans see themselves as deeply connected to the world, and yet also as part of spirit. That is why they journey in trance states to other realms to gather information and it is why today's shamans cross multiple boundaries through their work and activities. It is also why shamans use both analytical reasoning and intuitive insight. The modern shaman may not necessarily use trance to gather information, but may well travel to new realms where others do not typically tread and bring back information that seems unusual, contradictory, ambiguous, or paradoxical, at least until it is understood in its new context.

Consider the fractal and the shaman

There is another way in which modern science—physics, complexity theory, and chaos theory—are linked to the work of traditional shamans. As we explored earlier, new understandings in quantum physics have made physicists and other scientists deeply aware of the interconnectedness of all things in the universe at the quantum level. Greater understanding of the planet's ecological systems and their interrelatedness with human activity is similarly shifting understanding at the level of our experienced reality. An evolutionary perspective connects today's living beings of all sorts with their progenitors deeply in the past in what amounts to an unbroken line, because broken lines do not contain any currently living beings. Further, the "we are stardust" notion links us inextricably with all that is.

Shamans, who usually believe that everything has spirit, deeply understand these interrelationships and the connectedness of humans to other creatures, to nature, and to the universe. They tend to see things more holistically than many modern scientists and scholars do, who work with atomized fragments that break things into their smallest elements as a way of understanding them. A holistic way of understanding the world aligns with systems understanding and systems thinking and attempts to understand the dynamic complexity and interactivity that is essential to life—and found in all systems, including human social as well as ecological systems.

Traditional shamans understood "wholes" because the world they lived in did not fragment knowledge atomistically, as many, particularly Westerners, do today. While understanding fragments and breaking things into their fundamental units can be helpful, sometimes, particularly for dynamic systems and wicked problems, a more holistic or systemic understanding is the only way to begin to understand. Here is where the today's shaman can be helpful. Problems like sustainability, which some have called a superwicked problem because of its complexity, many moving parts, and the difficulty of resolving unsustainable practices, needs to be viewed holistically *as well as* being broken down into parts.

One scholar, Robert Perey,[98] has explored the sustainability problem in terms of an aspect of chaos theory called fractals, which I believe is related to the work of the modern shaman, particularly in dealing with complex systems problems. Fractals are infinitely complex structures, often organic and sometimes found in human systems, in which a repeating self-similar pattern exists at multiple levels or scales. In mathematics, fractals exhibit iterative qualities that generate multiple levels of structures, each one of which is similar to others. Sometimes they are said to be never-ending. The term was coined by the mathematician Benoit Mandelbrot (for whom one of the most famous such patterns is named). Many natural structures exhibit fractal characteristics, particularly where there is branching and pattern repetition, e.g., broccoli, pine cones, ice crystals formed on windows, lightning bolts, hurricanes, seashells, galaxies, river networks, trees, leaves, water drops, and air bubbles, to name a few.

Perey argues that fractals are "anything but linear," with all scales manifesting simultaneously. Many aspects of human life, including culture, organizing, and relationships can be said to have fractal qualities like self-similarity. He also argues that narrative—the sensemaking of the shaman—is vitally important to using fractal logic to help think about organizational and system change. Think for example of the network structure of some organizations, which can be viewed (and look much the same) at multiple levels, or the ways in which relationships in your life seem to repeat themselves over time with different people. Perey suggests that understanding fractals allows us—as change agents, for example, which many shamans are—to observe different levels or scales of reality at multiple levels and simultaneously. For example, the sustainability problem needs to be dealt with locally (e.g., in the home), in the community, nationally, regionally, and globally—and there are similar and highly complex issues—fractals—at each level, simultaneously, collaboratively, and separately.

Shamans know that understanding one level of a situation or problem helps with understanding the problem as a whole. As Perey notes, viewing something at one level or in one manifestation helps us understand the whole, because in fractal terms, the different levels are similar. Things that impact the wellbeing of a system at a given level will also affect the whole, because of the interrelationships and similarities that exist. The work of the shaman as sensemaker is particularly relevant in thinking about how fractals might be used for healing purposes—whether of individuals or systems. When you can tell a story that makes sense to others about one level of a fractal system, then you can begin to tell a story that impacts the whole—and generate new meanings that can, hopefully, enhance wellbeing overall; though, as Perey notes, not all new meanings or narratives have fractal qualities.[99] When they do, however, they can lend themselves to telling a bigger or more impactful story or narrative than would seem possible in a given situation.

Take, for example, the problem with growth—in my mind, the problem *is* growth. We normally assume that, in our economic system, growth is an underlying imperative. Yet it is this very imperative that is threatening the planet's ability to sustain human civilization as we know it. The growth imperative creates our expectation—in our current dominant economic and business narrative—that economic growth and hence business growth must continue exponentially at any cost. In this common narrative about growth, which does have fractal qualities, individuals must grow their jobs—selling ever more goods and services for example, so that departments can meet growth objectives, so that companies can meet their growth objectives, so that the industry can achieve new growth markers—ultimately so that the system as a whole can grow. But infinite growth on a finite planet, as ecologists make clear, is simply not possible.[100]

Changing the narrative about growth at any of these self-similar levels is part of the shaman's task as sensemaker. Shifting this narrative has the potential to change perspectives about the functions and purposes of businesses and their participants (or any other system or organized set of institutions)—and, importantly, the story about businesses' roles in the sustainability context. Only by changing the narrative and its underlying memes, core artifacts that build culture and shape our understanding of the world,[101] can the shaman begin to reshape our attitudes towards sustainability, businesses, and the imperatives that drive them. Understanding the fractal qualities of certain narratives, like the growth narrative, can help today's shamans, particularly those people who are intellectual shamans, to begin to shape a new narrative. This new narrative needs to be more holistic, Earth-centric, and geared towards the wellbeing of the planet's creatures, including humankind, and its ecosystems in all their manifestations.

As Perey argues, "Working with fractal perspectives lends itself to working with and understanding dynamic systems."[102] If we think about the changes that are needed to bring about a sustainable enterprise economy, perhaps the idea of using fractals can help us cope with the magnitude of the change needed. If changes needed are self-similar, then starting at a small scale—in homes, for example—can be a first step that anyone can take to help build a logic that moves us towards implementing sustainability initiatives in organizations. Then steps that are local, community-wide, state- or province-wide, and ultimately national and planetary can be taken using what has been learned at small levels of the fractal space. Similarly, fractal logic helps us understand that wherever we intervene we make a difference to the whole. That is: if we work at whatever level seems most workable to create greater sustainability, wellbeing, or whatever our goals are as shamanic practitioners hoping to heal the world, the changes that we make have the potential to spread out into self-similar initiatives at the rest of the levels as well. The point is: understanding fractal logic as part of a change or sustainability strategy lets us know we have to start somewhere to achieve whole-system change—because the whole is interconnected, dynamic, and of a piece, and wherever we start is the right place.

Complexity, chaos, emergence, and the shaman

As we have seen, emerging ideas in philosophy and science about what consciousness actually is and how the elements of our world are connected support the reality that "subjective" data and experience are important in understanding our systems and how we might help heal them. These understandings help us also recognize that any understanding, idea, or conceptualization is part of a process of what is called "emergence," which is basically the ways in which ideas or other things come into view. The process of emergence emphasizes the ways in which patterns, similarities, and more complex or larger entities come into being from more fundamental units.[103]

"Emergence" simply means that actions and activities create new interactions, patterns, and outcomes, even new and more complex systems. Not all of the elements are present in the original actors or systems because they tend to form a new whole that cannot necessarily be reduced to its parts as they emerge. Emergence is part of so-called "self-organizing systems" that are present in complex systems. For example, life itself is sometimes considered by biologists to be an emergent process, in which various elements (cells, atoms, molecules, proteins, etc.)

come together to form a new entity (living being) that can no longer be "reduced" or taken apart into its component parts and retain its identity as a living being. That is, the new system that emerged from its component elements is something more than and different than the elements when they are separated from the new system or pattern. The whole, from the perspective of emergence, is something more than the sum of its parts. The whole, that is, has an integral quality to it that cannot be subdivided and still retain the essence of whatever that "whole" is.

Complexity theory or complexity science, as it is variously called, is an approach to understanding complex systems, which are non-linear in their dynamics, highly interactive, and have emergent properties, as well as, sometimes, self-organization. In dealing with individuals', communities', or societies' problems, shamans are necessarily addressing complex systems, and need to understand the realities of dealing with such systems. Those realities mean that there is little that is specifically predictable, although as complexity scientists point out and is discussed above, patterns typically repeating at multiple levels or layers, i.e., fractals, can frequently be detected in complex systems. Since such systems are frequently "chaotic" in the mathematical sense, they are inherently non-linear. The non-linearity of complex systems means that, despite recognizable patterns, the specific next event cannot be predicted with any degree of certainty.

Complexity theory deals with multiple, dynamic interactions, from which sometimes emerge relatively simple patterns, which are non-deterministic and cannot be accurately and precisely predicted. Sometimes very simply interactions among a few elements can yield highly complex patterns that show up as fractals. Examples of natural systems that exhibit such fractal qualities include mountain ranges, lightning, snowflakes, and many crystals. In social and organizational life we can see similarities that the shaman can sometimes recognize and work with. For example, as we have seen earlier, departmental structures in an organization can mirror the broader organizational structure, which itself may mirror broader industry structures (e.g., bureaucratic structures replicating bureaucratic structures within existing structures, or network structures similarly replicating within networked contexts).

Complexity theory is related to chaos theory, which is the study of emergence patterns from very complicated information interacting interdependently. Complex and chaotic systems are non-linear, highly interactive, and dynamic. Chaotic systems, however, typically arise out of the repeated application of simple rules and dynamics, while complexity arises from the interactions of numerous sub-units. Both chaotic and complex systems are what theorists call sensitive to initial conditions, meaning that very small differences that occur in interactions after the initial state can generate very large ultimate systemic differences. Complex systems are frequently seen to be self-organizing in that they generate new and relatively stable system conditions, e.g., the complexity of the Earth considered as Gaia, i.e., as itself a living entity as ecologist and futurist James Lovelock has named it.[104]

Complex systems persist in a state that complexity theorists call far from equilibrium or the edge of chaos, which simply means that they never settle into a fully stable condition and could devolve into what in colloquial terms we consider chaos to be. Such systems are subject to dynamism and change, even sudden state changes that can create dramatically new conditions or situations.

Complex systems are also subject to what evolutionary biologists would call co-evolutionary processes, in which the actions of one organism help to shape the context in which it exists and to which it must then respond. We can see much the same experience of co-evolution in organizational and other human processes. Just think at the level of interpersonal relationships for a moment. If one individual is angry at another, that shapes how she or he acts toward the other person and triggers a variety of responses from the other individual. Together, these interactions shape the interpersonal context in which these two individuals exist and how they relate to each other, and can also affect the way that others entering into their "space" experience both individuals, their relationship, and the culture of whatever situation they find themselves in. Similar dynamics apply at different levels of analysis.

Emergence is intimately linked to the science of complexity, because emergent processes inevitably result in complex systems with multiple interacting parts. Indeed, there are so many interactions that the ways in which any of them interact, i.e., how they are connected is indeterminate—and inherently unpredictable. In such systems, small shifts or changes at some initial stage can generate very large changes later on in what is known as the butterfly effect. The butterfly effect is an important element of chaos theory, which meteorologist Edward Lorenz[105] articulated in the 1960s. It states that the flapping of a butterfly's wings in South America can potentially generate shifts in weather patterns large enough to emerge as a hurricane elsewhere in the world weeks later. In other words, very small changes in initial conditions can have very large repercussions later on in complex systems. The exact path that the system takes, because of changes that can be very small, is not predetermined, nor is it predictable. Patterns can be seen, but specific predictions cannot be made in such circumstances. Examples of complex systems include weather, crystal structures, biological organisms, natural ecologies, and social systems of all sorts.

Today's shaman understands these realities and complexities. The shaman's job, in one sense, is to help shape the state of the future system as it emerges, in a process that MIT intellectual shaman and professor Otto Scharmer, who has developed a change theory that he calls "Theory U," calls "letting come"[106] and I call "allowing." Shamans accomplish this healing task as change agents through their connecting and sensemaking roles. In connecting, they bring together ideas and insights in new ways. In sensemaking, they are reshaping the story or narrative that the patient, community, or society is telling itself about whatever issue needs resolution, which is a core aspect of the healing that the shaman does.[107] But they can only make such sense of what is happening when they have a systemic perspective on the emergent patterns and intersections in the system. Shamans in this sensemaking sense can give "nudges" in new directions through their new narratives, reshaping relevant mythologies.

7

The shaman as leader today

How can and do shamans work in the world today, a world dominated by scientific and economic memes that focus us on rational, logical, and scientific explanations for just about everything? Since shamans work from non-ordinary reality—intuition, instinct, creative impulses, and beyond-the-self sources, the work of today's shaman is not necessarily tied to the rituals, ceremonies, and practices of traditional shamans. At least, in my view, it need not be. Of course, if those practices appeal to you and work for you, then by all means use them. At its core, shamanism is about using what works to heal ourselves, our world, and our relationships to others and to that world. The key to doing the shaman's work is to find what feeds your soul—and what the world needs to heal. They are endless places to begin.

This last chapter explores the ways in which shamans act as leaders and change agents. I also argue that business and other leaders, acting as shamans, could and would take a considerably different perspective on their work—and that the world would be better off if they did.

Shaping the shift and the shamanic leader

Many of our organizations, communities, and institutions today need radical transformation to cope with the problems that the world is facing, not least of which are sustainability, climate change, and growing inequity. As a result, a major question for today's shamanic leader is can this capability for shapeshifting help in bringing about needed changes? That is, can shamanic leaders not just shapeshift, as discussed in Chapter 5, but actually *shape the shift* that is needed to bring about a sustainable social, political, and economic system? Shaping the shift is a core activity of the change agent and the leader: building a better future for all.

Shaping the shift draws on each of the core functions of the shaman: healing, connecting, and sensemaking. The first step is to recognize that there are problems in the world that need to be healed—and then to set out to shape changes that can actually bring about needed changes in a direction that is more inclusive of all, more equitable, and sustainable. Through the healing function, the shamanic leader recognizes that "business as usual" itself, whether in business, government, or communities, can sometimes be what is problematic. This insight triggers knowledge that doing "business," whatever the business or institution/organization might be, in new ways is called for because of the troubled times, because of lack of sustainability, or many of the other significant problems facing humankind on the planet today.

Achieving this awareness is no mean feat for leaders who have been successful in whatever business-as-usual environment they operate in. Such awareness demands the shaman's ability to see beyond one's own self-interest to the whole—whether that is the whole enterprise, community, or society . . . or even the whole planet. It also requires a willingness to admit that business-as-usual is what is causing problems, and then to be willing to take steps needed to make changes (shape the shift) for the better through whatever means the leader has at her or his disposal. In short, achieving this awareness demands shapeshifting to envision what might or needs to be rather than what is. Then it demands shaping the shift—making changes—to achieve a new, healthier system.

As connectors, shamanic leaders interested in shaping the shift have to connect the dots around the current system. That is, they need to be able to understand the systemic influences that are creating and sustaining the problematic current situation. What, for example, is the incentive system doing to shape current outcomes in an organization? What dynamics and forces are at play in fostering how the system responds to change? Where are sources of resistance and why is the resistance occurring? Who are potential allies in a change process, and who are likely to be resistors to the end? What will attract needed resources for the change—and, indeed, what are the resources that need to be attracted? Such questions can help a shamanic leader shape the necessary shift—what my friend and co-author Malcolm McIntosh has called the "necessary transition" to a sustainable enterprise economy[108] that is needed to build a more equitable and sustainable world.

Armed with this understanding, which is a form of holistic systems thinking, the shapeshifting leader can ask, "What role do I or does my enterprise or institution play in creating this problem?" and "Where are there levers that could shift the system?" Sometimes shaping the shift involves creating a new business model for businesses, designing a social enterprise, developing new ways of interacting with stakeholders to create better relationships. Sometimes it simply involves listening to what is needed from others and helping them empower themselves to act constructively. Other times, finding the leverage for change is simpler, involving rethinking the reward system within an enterprise that creates incentives for problematic behaviors. There are many potential points of leverage that can be explored depending on the specific circumstance. Once the leverage within the current institution or situation is understood, changes in its potential impact on the broader system can be explored as part of the connecting task of the shaman. Organizations that take the lead in shaping the shift can then serve as role models for other enterprises, much as Unilever under the guidance of CEO Paul Polman—who is surely a shamanic leader of today—is doing in attempting to transform Unilever into a sustainable company.

Importantly, to shape the shift, the shamanic leader needs to understand what the memes, or core ideas and fundamental cultural units, are that are shaping the way people perceive the enterprise or institution. Even more fundamentally, to shape the shift involves uncovering the memes that drive understanding of the system as a whole and, when necessary, shaping the shift by actually creating new memes better suited to current conditions. Working at the level of memes is an important and frequently overlooked aspect of shaping the shift, because the memes that we buy into shape our understanding of and relationship to the world around us. A brief explanation may help.

Memes are images, symbols, phrases, words, and ideas that shape our attitudes, belief systems, and, importantly, the stories that we tell ourselves about how the world (or this institution/ situation) operates.[109] They are essentially the building blocks of the narratives and stories that shape our worldviews, attitudes, and ultimately our behaviors. Memes, in my view, are fundamental to shaping the shift—and often overlooked.[110]

If we consider for a moment the memes that shape how we understand the role of business today, perhaps this idea will be clearer. For example, if we understand the purpose of a company (a popular meme) to be solely to "maximize shareholder wealth," as some economics would have it, then our view of the social and ecological role of that enterprise is likely to be limited. If we firmly believe that markets are "free," as the current dominant economic narrative has it, then we will most likely want to keep them "free." If, instead, we build a set of memes that suggests that enterprises fundamentally need to work with the best interests of numerous stakeholder groups, or to serve societal interests in ecologically sustainable ways, our view of how that enterprise works and operates in societies will shift dramatically. If, instead, we recognize that markets are shaped by governmental policies and social norms that keep them stable and trustworthy, our attitudes towards both markets and the governments that support them will shift accordingly—and so will our behaviors. That shift in memes and associated narratives is a core aspect of shaping the shift. Such shiftshaping through new, more realistic, and holistic meme development and narrative construction is a fundamental aspect of the sensemaking task of today's shaman.[111]

The sensemaking capacity of the shaman in this sense is perhaps the most important task involved in shaping the shift, e.g., towards a more sustainable enterprise economy. Through the sensemaking task, the shamanic leader uses new memes to develop a new narrative or story about the institution that can begin to shift the way people perceive and interact with that institution, organization, or entity. Further, using the power of envisioning the future, today's shamanic leaders can play central roles in shaping the shift by exploring the impact and replication of different new memes that shape our understanding of enterprise.

Shamanic leaders can in their sensemaking role create new and powerful memes and visions that can help both themselves and others imagine how our troubled world could be different—and how we might get there. To do so, however, means using the other two capabilities of the effective shaman—the healing capability that orients us towards building a better world, and the connecting function that allows us to make the necessary links across systems and understandings and which can help us shape new narratives and memes.

Shapeshifting new memes and narratives

Whether it is through storytelling, reframing the situation or an individual or community's relationship to its world, or simply helping others understand what happening and why, the shaman uses insights gathered from any number of sources to help others understand and cope better with the world around them. By generating new or reframing old memes that influence the way people understand and relate to their world, today's shamans can use their gifts in powerful ways.

Memes, as the fundamental building blocks of culture, values, norms, and many other aspects of societies,[112] can be words (think of how the word "awesome" has shifted meaning). They can be phrases (think of colloquial sayings like "a dime a dozen"), or images and brands (think of the Nike "swoosh" or the Coca-Cola bottle and logo). They can be iconic art (think of artist Andy Warhol's Marilyn Monroe pictures or the first few notes of Beethoven's Fifth Symphony). They can be symbols (think of the Christian cross or the Chinese yin–yang symbol). Importantly, memes can be ideas (think of the currently dominant memes around business, for example, of maximizing shareholder wealth or free markets, mentioned above). When memes combine into sets or groups, they can become narratives or stories (sometimes called memeplexes).[113]

These narratives and stories comprised of memes are important ways in which we relate to the world around us. Such stories and narratives provide a context for how we understand our relationship to the world around us, what we believe is true and what is false by shaping our attitudes, belief systems, and ideologies, and, ultimately, as a consequence, our behaviors. For example, in our modern world, most educated observers tend to believe that science is the best and sometimes only way to understand the world around us. Although science, of course, provides tremendous insights, shamans implicitly know that there are other ways that we learn and know things as well. Hence telling different stories can help us reshape the world around us. Indeed, one of the missing elements in most change efforts is that they fail to deal with the level of memes and the stories that develop out of those memes; hence people have no framework to hang various change initiatives around.[114]

Remember that a core element of the healing task of the shaman is to reframe dis-eased or dis-ordered cultural mythologies
so that the patient can get better. In the case of our societies and
social systems, the "patient" is a collective entity, dis-eased and
dis-ordered because of lack of sustainability, inequity, insecurity,
intolerance, or any number of other ills. Both new narratives
and new types of actions, connecting across systems and beginning to collaborate in new ways, are needed to reform and
reframe these systems. Today's shaman as change agent can
undertake both of these types of activities.

Shamans understand that memes inspire others when they
resonate, because they help people understand the world in new
or different ways. When they resonate, they get repeated by others (most likely somewhat transforming in the process). That is,
because we are human, stories (unlike images and words) tend
to change as they pass from person to person. Still, memes and
narratives help us develop a way of interacting with the world
around us and with others, because they shape how we understand our world (and others). Creating and promulgating memes
that help to heal the "story" that surrounds a given community
is an important function of the shaman as sensemaker.

As noted earlier, scholars Peter Frost and Carolyn Egri called
the sensemaking role of the shaman spiritual leadership when
they discussed the change agent (organizational development
specialist) as a shaman. Doing such work, shamans use memes
to shape new narratives and stories that both heal what is broken in the current story and help people understand and relate
to their world in different ways. In Indigenous cultures, shamans do play a central role in their communities as spiritual
leaders, because they help to shape the narratives or stories that
connect people to each other and to the world around them

through their work as healers. It is the sensemaking role that allows them to do this, and the spiritual aspect comes about because, fundamentally, sensemaking is about making meaning, which has significant overtones of spirituality. Most of us seek meaning in our lives: a core aspect of spirituality. The narratives about our cultures and how we fit into those cultures can be helpful guides in developing a sense of purpose, life direction, and work and play that allows us to make whatever contributions our particular gifts allow.

Going back to the idea of memes, then, it is the shamans among us who help shape new memes that draw attention both to what is wrong with existing narratives and stories and provide the basis for creating new stories that help us realign ourselves, our communities, and the world with different principles.

Today's shamans also act in the world. There are endless ways and multiple levels at which you, acting in your healing capacity as shaman, can begin this work. Think about the many ills of the world and think about what bothers you most where you might be able to do something. Is it lack of sufficient beauty or "green" space in your neighborhood? Build a garden, create a sculpture that beautifies, clean up a dead zone, or in other ways create beauty in your home, neighborhood, community, or in the world. Is it a question of unethical practices in your workplace? Find ways to open up conversations that shift the culture, reward system, and practices in the firm towards more ethical and trustworthy interactions. Does inequality, mass incarceration, drug abuse, social injustice, or something else along these lines trouble you? Does the current state of the political or governmental system concern you? Get active and use your shamanic gifts to bring about the changes, visibility, and change of narrative that are needed. Is unsustainability a problem for you?

Begin to work collaboratively with others who are dealing with these issues.

Whatever you do, you need to begin somewhere to exert your shamanic power and use your gifts. We are all drawn to different things and bring our own unique skills, talents, and shamanic insights and gifts to what we do. All of these activities take some degree of courage and certainly initiative. That is why becoming and being a shaman is not always easy, and why a steady and ongoing practice is a necessary support.

Shamanic vs. "tough" leaders

Not all leaders are shamanic. There is a lot of talk in the world today about a certain type of leader, who seems to be admired and in some cases even lionized: the tough leader. You know the type. We see them in business and in politics quite a lot.

This leader is the one who screams at people in impatience when things don't go his or her way, the one who has to have his (typically "his" but not always) way or you can take the highway. Some of these purported leaders even resort to calling people who disagree with or question them derisive and insulting names. Like spoiled children, they sometimes have tantrums when they or their ideas are not immediately accepted. Through their actions and antics, they disrespect the integrity and full personhood of others, assuming that others are present only to meet their, the leader's, needs and wants. Indeed, some such leaders are prominent political figures. Others head up big companies or other major institutions. We have probably all encountered at least one such leader.

Because of their drive, ability to understand how the "game" of business, politics, or institutional work is played, no matter what the consequences, and their willingness to do whatever it takes to succeed, such individuals are frequently lauded in the business press for their "toughness." But what does this toughness mean? Some scholars and even business magazines have made a link between such "tough" leaders and socio- or psychopaths. According to Jon Ronson, who has studied such individuals in leadership capacities, psychopaths are individuals with no conscience or empathy for others. They are manipulative, deceitful, yet are often quite charming (which can help explain their success). They can also be delusional about their abilities and impacts.[115] Not a nice picture.

The "toughness" of such leaders supposedly helps them get results. Indeed, some of these people do get results, at least in the short term, because they drive their subordinates hard and have high (sometimes unrealistic) expectations. Mostly, they get results because subordinates, co-workers, and even colleagues fear their wrath should these individuals be disappointed in outcomes or challenged in any way. Sometimes, they are inconsistent in their demands, confusing subordinates and making their work lives very difficult because expectations keep shifting.

Such leaders are, in my view, the opposite of shamanic leaders. Shamanic leaders are generative, supportive, and aim for healing not harming others. Shamanic leaders have empathic qualities, as well as a strong ethical stance that enables them to focus on healing and the ultimate ends of their work rather than short-term means get simply get things done. They value other people and the communities in which they operate, not to mention the natural world around us, which is the source of all we have and value in the end. They can set high standards without abusing or demeaning others, because they are internally healed themselves, because they have faced their own fears, and understand how to help others in facing theirs.

While it is certainly conceivable that some "tough" leaders can develop the healing, connecting, and sensemaking agenda associated with the shaman, most of them are far from the shaman in leadership behaviors. We might, in fact, call them sorcerers, i.e., shamans who turn their power to selfish or problematic purposes. In my view, "tough" leaders are too frequently abusive bullies, who inspire nothing but fear.

While fear is an important and necessary response in dangerous situations, enabling people to figure out ways to protect themselves, constant fear in work and community situations creates stress, which leads to all sorts of problems. Think of terms associated with fear: panic, trepidation, apprehension, breaking into a cold sweat, dread, terror, alarm, and aversion, cringing, horror, shuddering, among many others. How creative, innovative, empathic, or productive can people really be when these types of words describe their state of mind? How productive, insightful, and innovative are they? Fear hurts people because it limits what they are willing to do as well as the creativity and innovativeness of their responses.

Fear, as noted earlier, is associated with the "fight or flight" response, which is a state of hyper-arousal associated with acute stress. While fight or flight is a healthy response in emergency situations, it is unhealthy for people to live in such a high state of stress for long periods of time, as stress is known to cause both physical and emotional problems. Over time, fear shrinks people, makes them smaller than they are psychically and emotionally (and sometimes even physically, as the term shrinking with fear implies). Because they are afraid to make mistakes or because they are vulnerable to criticism or abuse, fearful people find it hard to fully "show up" in situations where they have to face an abusive boss or leader. They find it hard to do their best and most generative work under these circumstances, because criticism or other demeaning behavior from the leader is always a distinct possibility.

Rather than working from inducing a state of fear as "tough" leaders do, shamanic leaders work from a place of love. Love helps others become bigger than they might otherwise be. The shamanic leader, in contrast to the abusive one, inspires creative energy through the healing of others, through storytelling, and by connecting ideas, issues, and people who have not previously connected. There is a generative quality to the work of the shaman that simply cannot exist in the context of abusive use of power. While the power of the shaman can sometimes generate awe, the basis of that power is not fear but love.

As noted, you can live in one of two states—love or fear. The "tough" leader leads from and in fear. The shamanic leader leads from love. Love is generative, productive, and giving. Fear is the opposite. Similarly, leaders can induce either of these states and, if they wish to get the best out of subordinates and colleagues, the approach from a place of love is likely to be best.

Love: dignity for everything

Because shamans believe that everything has spirit, that belief informs the way that they treat others and the world around them, including other living creatures and the natural environment itself. Fundamentally, what this belief means is that true shamans treat others and the world around them with love, and as if they had inherent dignity. Dignity means a person, institution, or part of nature has worthiness in and of itself. Dignity is a quality of being worthy or honor, simply because someone or something is, not because of what the person, institution, or nature has accomplished.[116] How different that attitude is from the normal way that many of us treat other people who may be different in some way from ourselves? Or how we treat nature itself?

We humans are deeply embedded with others, nature, and the universe as a whole. The concept of dignity can help make this deep interconnection more meaningful. Harvard University's Donna Hicks, author of a book entitled *Dignity*, has a perspective on dignity and respect that strikes me as distinctly shamanic. Hicks writes that every person is born with dignity and deserves to be treated with dignity. If we view others and the world around us as imbued with spirit, that perspective automatically focuses us on treating others and the world, including all aspects of nature, as if they had inherent dignity. When we see dignity as an integral part of others and nature, there is less chance that we will mistreat or misuse either.

Hicks differentiates dignity from respect. Dignity is inherent and we all have it. Dignity is an integral condition of life, which is the quality of being *worthy* of honor or respect. She would argue that everyone is born worthy of such respect, i.e., with dignity, simply for their personhood. We are all, that is, worthy of being accorded dignity, of living a decent life, of connecting with others in mutually respectful ways. Shamans would agree that all living beings and nature as a whole, because it is imbued with spirit, also have dignity and deserve to be treated accordingly.

Respect, in contrast, is something that must be earned, Hicks points out. So while we all have an obligation to treat others without injuring their dignity, we need to respect only those others who have earned that respect. Respect means deep admiration for something or something, and derives from their abilities, qualities, or achievements. If you respect someone or something, you hold it in high esteem because of what it stands for, what it has done, or what it means to you. But even when you don't have respect for someone or some part of nature, it still has inherent worth—or dignity.

You might, for example, have respect for a politician or leader because of what she or he has accomplished for your community or nation. Or, if that individual has done something injurious to you or others—you might lose respect for him or her. For instance, it is hard for me to respect politicians and bosses who abuse and bully citizens, the press, or others: the "tough" bosses discussed in the previous section. I believe that such individuals still have dignity and need to be treated as people, as philosophers might say, as ends in themselves, not as means to an end. But if they are mistreating others, I don't need to respect them. The same can be said of an institution. If an institution, e.g., a church, government, or business, has institutionally done or permitted egregious things to happen because of some systemic failure, that institution does not deserve respect. But as an institution, it still carries dignity.

Affronts to dignity are serious and hurtful. Affronts to dignity are the often unspoken root of many conflicts and other problems in our world: that is, things that need healing. Hicks recognized this important reality in her global work in conflict resolution, and works tirelessly to ensure that all parties to conflict are aware of the ways in which their words, ideas, and actions might cause dignity violations to others. When dignity violations occur, it is important to correct them, so that people can experience their full personhood, rather than feeling demeaned or diminished as they do in a context of dignity violations.

The implications of a love- and dignity-based perspective on the world around us, a shamanic perspective, are stunning. In the West, many believe that nature is there only for human exploitation and that we humans are somehow separate from nature. Holding that belief puts humans at the center of the planet (and, probably, the universe as well). But the reality is that human beings and the societies that we create are deeply interconnected and interdependent with nature. Humans cannot survive without the resources that nature provides—and to make our societies and civilizations healthy, we humans, who now have so much impact on the world that we are causing climate change and sustainability crises, need to understand this reality.

What if we viscerally and deeply understood, as shamans, that we are connected to all the other living and non-living beings, and, indeed, to our universe as a whole? What if that understanding led us to realize that there is some way in which we cannot separate ourselves from the rest of the world? How would such a recognition change our relationships with other people—even those people quite different from ourselves? Or with nature and its many creatures? Or even with the rocks, mountains, trees, and ecosystems that comprise nature?

Happily enough, as we saw in Chapter 6, modern physics supports this core shamanic belief about interconnectedness. Somehow, though, this insight has not penetrated to our everyday understanding. As noted earlier in talking about Joni Mitchell's song "Woodstock," everything we are comprised of, all of the particles and atoms that make up our beings—and everything else—was present at the so-called Big Bang in which our universe was created nearly 14 billion years ago. The atoms and other particles that comprise any given thing existed in many other forms through those billions of years, making us fundamentally part of those other forms—i.e., of the universe itself.

It is this essential connectedness and our interdependence with everything that exists at the quantum level that is what shamans find in other creatures and elements. This connectedness is, I believe, what shamans calls Spirit. It is in recognizing such Spirit within other beings and entities and in the universe as a whole, that healing can potentially be found. Because shamans believe that everything is imbued with spirit, they accord dignity and respect other creatures and natural elements in ways that we in Western cultures sometimes do not. Shamans inherently respect animals, plants, bodies of water, mountains, trees, and even human-made items, because the elements that make up human-made items come from that same connected universe.

For the Western mind, where body and mind, never mind spirit, are viewed as separate, these beliefs can seem strange indeed. Yet advances in quantum physics are reshaping our understanding of the world and suggest that it is at least possible that shamans are not too far off in their perspectives. The implications of this perspective are stunning. If we were to recognize spirit or connectedness between and within all of nature and her creatures, including ourselves, wouldn't that change our attitude towards both other living creatures and non-living ones? Such a fundamental respect would be a far cry from the Western world's treatment of nature as something to be exploited and used for the sake of humanity. It might return us to the shamanic perspective that we are connected to our universe and to each other, a perspective that seems sorely missing in much of modern society.

The shamanic perspective inherently recognizes that we are all in this world (and universe) together. As we struggle to deal with a world that seems increasingly fragmented and troubled, recognizing our connectedness is an important step in changing our attitudes towards unlike "others" as well as towards nature. Such an attitude or mindset shift could potentially be important to humans in dealing with issues of global peace, for greater sustainability, and for getting along with others in general, at both the local and global levels.

In some very real way, shamans know that what happens to one of us happens to all of us. Perhaps by incorporating a shamanic perspective, we can begin the (shamanic) mindset shift that is needed to change our world for the better, as discussed next.

Dignity, business, our economic system . . . and today's shaman

The idea of dignity and spirit in all can be further extended to considerations about how businesses and other organizations operate in societies today. Believing that there is dignity in the world around us, in nature's creatures, in other people, and all aspects of Earth, creates a very different mindset than is typical of much Western thought. This difference is particularly evident when we consider today's dominant business and economic system.

Businesses today are oriented toward exploiting as much of nature as possible for the benefit of the "owners" (shareholders) of the business, fostering as much growth as possible, combined with an efficiency and productivity orientation, ideas that apply no matter the costs (or what are called "externalities" by economists) to other aspects of the system, including nature. In today's system, exploitation of natural resources and people is commonplace. It is evidenced in our blowing off tops of mountains to get at minerals, growing interest in "fracking" to extract inaccessible energy resources, exploitation of human beings through problematic global supply chains and slave or near-slave labor in some developing countries, whose work benefits the developed world in the form of low-cost goods. It is evidenced, among other ways, in fracking, and the pumping of toxic chemicals into products and, as a by-product, the natural environment, among many other negative impacts of the current production and economic system.

Imagine a more shamanic approach to business and economy that accorded dignity to other living beings—animal and plant, elements of nature, and the Earth itself. Scholars Thomas Donaldson and James P. Walsh have argued for a new theory of business that would alter business purpose and our economic system as a whole.[117] In their theory, Donaldson and Walsh argue that what they term "collective value" should be the goal of businesses, with the important caveat that there should be no dignity violations in the doing of business. Although Donaldson and Walsh limit their conception of dignity violations to human beings, they do consider the possibility of according dignity to all living beings, to "non-living" aspects of nature, and to the Earth (Gaia) itself, but ultimately focus the according of dignity on humans.

A shamanic perspective would make this very elaboration explicit by according dignity to all living creatures. Imagine for a moment that spirit does reside in everything. With this belief, the shamanic leader, policy maker, business person, and activist accords dignity to trees, plants, and all kinds of other living beings, to natural elements like rocks, mountains, lakes, rivers, plains, and forests, and to the Earth as a whole. Such things are perceived as valuable in and of themselves, just as human beings are, albeit with perhaps (in some cases considerably) less awareness of their own existence than humans have. If embedded into our economic and business thinking, such a shamanic perspective would be very different from the exploitative, rent-seeking, efficiency-and-growth-at-whatever-the-costs model of business that dominates our world today. Businesses—and the rest of us—would treat nature and its beings very differently than many of us currently do.

By extending the idea of dignity to Earth, its creatures, and its natural elements, our ideas about how businesses create value for the whole would shift as part of the shapeshifting practice of leaders discussed earlier. Through such a revisioning, the collective value that Donaldson and Walsh imagine at the core of a new theory of business would encompass the world around us in entirely new ways. This shamanic perspective applied to businesses would shift our ideas about how to produce the goods and services that we need, and what care and responsibilities we ought to take in the production process.

Importantly, people wherever they are in the world and whatever their status, would be treated differently. Businesses would be asked in such a system to treat all people with dignity to generate common or collective value (also called the common good), no matter where they were in the supply and distribution chains. Notably, this orientation towards people as ends in themselves is a fundamental precept of ethics. Fully implemented, it would, for example, mean that everyone deserves working conditions that allow their dignity to survive. It would mean no more exploitative working conditions that demean and dehumanize people. Workers in global supply chains would have to be paid a living wage—a wage that allows them to support a family, live in decent conditions, and eat nutritious and sufficient food, for example. They would also have to be accorded dignity in the nature of the work they are asked to do. Dignity would apply to how their bosses and co-workers treat them, no matter who they were, where they were living and working, or what type of work they were doing. Even workers and employees in industrialized nations could expect to be treated better than many currently are, with reasonable working hours, respect from their bosses, and adequate working conditions and facilities.

A shamanic approach that accords dignity to all in business would also suggest that many of today's "modern" practices would need to be rethought. For example, practices around agricultural production, animal husbandry (e.g., cattle and chicken production practices), meat processing, fishing practices like trawling that result in overfishing and devastation of large ocean tracts, and the use of chemical fertilizers and pesticides would, among many others, would be subject to change. Treating the land with dignity would, for example, mean much more organically based agricultural practices, including far less monocultural production practices, far less use of chemical fertilizers and pesticides, as examples. More organic, and perhaps traditional, methods of farming might be better suited to treating the land, the topsoil, and its many living creatures, with dignity. Such approaches would likely also provide jobs for people who need them, and there is mounting evidence that such approaches are not only productive for the land, but can also produce food of higher nutritional value and in sufficient quantities to feed the world's population.

Animal husbandry practices, which have received widespread notoriety for their cruelty and abuses, would also need to change in a more dignity-based approach. If animals were treated as if they have spirit and dignity, then mass production techniques that raise and keep them in inhumane conditions, use artificial means of growing and fattening them as quickly as possible, and attempt to keep them "healthy" in the inherently unhealthful conditions in which they are grown would have to shift. While people would most likely continue to eat animal products, a more shamanic approach would honor the spirits of these creatures and treat them respectfully even when they were destined to be food products. Native Americans, for example, offered prayers to and for their prey, and gave them thanks for the food that they provided, when they were to be slaughtered. Further, they used all parts of the slaughtered animals, with very little going to waste. What a difference such approaches would be from the horrendous conditions of mass production slaughterhouses described in books like *Fast Food Nation*[118] and *The Omnivore's Dilemma*.[119]

Further, if business leaders accorded dignity to nature itself, then the land, our rivers, our mountains, lakes, and plains would be treated very differently than they are today. If you believe that a river, for example, is a living entity in some way, then the prospect of dumping toxic waste into it becomes considerably less appealing. The same could be said of the way that companies treat the atmosphere and other sources of pollution that might be spewed out of factories. If mountains were considered to have integrity in and of themselves, i.e., dignity, the blowing off their tops and dumping the residue in nearby valleys and streams would quickly become a thing of the past. The desecration of land that occurs from mine dumps would have to cease and new ways of finding the resources that are needed would have to be developed. This shift could foster a whole wave of ingenuity and innovation in business practices that become humanized and more "human" for the planet in the best sense of the word.

There are many, many other implications of a more shamanically rooted, dignity-based approach to business and economics. There are business people today who recognize the dignity violations to people, creatures, and Earth and try to work *with* nature and people rather than exploit them. Biodynamic farming, organic farming, companies that truly value their employees and treat workers throughout their supply chains well, demanding that all suppliers live up to high standards, for example, bring this more shamanic perspective to business.

Perhaps taking on this type of shamanic perspective is unrealistic today, but hopefully not. A shamanic perspective suggests that we need to accept that many of today's practices generate numerous dignity violations to people, other living beings, and nature as a whole. It means that we need to recognize the many sustainability and climate change issues with the current linear, raw-material-to-landfill approaches of most of today's industrialized processes that characterize our economic system. Adopting a shamanic perspective, we might be able to recognize that, if humanity is to thrive in the future, it must do so in accord with principles of love and dignity for all people, living beings, and all manifestations of nature. The shamanic perspective can help all of us to understand the new realities facing our world.

example, in addition to consumption expenditures, which are measured in GDP, it uses a weighted indicator of private consumption that takes income inequality into account. It also adds in non-paid (non-market) services (like childcare, eldercare, volunteer and community building activities) that go uncounted in GDP. GPI subtracts out both the costs of natural deterioration (e.g., use of non-renewable resources that cannot be replaced in a lifetime) and defensive environmental costs (e.g., costs of protecting the natural environment or neutralizing a decrease in environmental quality). Finally, it adds in the increase in stock share prices and balance-of-trade measures.

Measures like GPI, if more widely adopted than they presently are, could be used to assess national levels of wellbeing. GPI far better reflects the shamanic perspective that nature needs to be valued of and for itself, without respect to how it can be used (or exploited) by humans, than does GDP, although even the GPI and similar measures are still far from perfect measures of the dignity of all. Ultimately, they could more accurately reflect that state of wellbeing in a society and even globally. Collective value at the company and community levels needs a similar kind of logic and new and innovative ways to think about whether and how a company or other enterprise (e.g., social or political) contributes to collective value.

Shamans and the paradox of sustainable development

Sometimes what seems like a paradox can simply be an expression that goes against what is accepted as the common wisdom. As we have seen in the previous chapter, today's shamans understand and can live with such ambiguities and contradic-tions—paradoxes. In the current system of economics, busi-ness, and production, businesses and other enterprises extract resources from the natural environment, manufacture some-thing, sell it, users use the product, then (mostly) throw it away, often into a landfill where it sits permanently, sometimes leach-ing toxins into the ground depending on how well designed the landfill is.

For many, "business as usual" seems to be common sense, since it is how things have been done since our industrial era began and is familiar. Thus, this system seems reasonable. Yet sustainability experts tell us that this system, which on the sur-face seems to have given so much to so many in terms of eco-nomic development, is not ecologically sustainable. Many sus-tainability experts say that we need to move towards what they call a circular economy, in which our current linear system transforms to what ecologists call a "waste equals food" sys-tem. Waste equals food means that nothing actually goes to waste because what is waste for one system becomes food for another.[121] Such a transformation may be necessary to avoid the processes of "development" and the demand for economic "growth" on a finite planet that are now creating significant long-term problems for humanity.

Our current production-system business operates in what amounts to a linear path from resources to landfill. This process has delivered significant economic development on the one hand, bringing many people out of poverty and providing liveli-hoods for them. On the other hand, and paradoxically, this sys-tem is creating what may be a crisis for humanity, a crisis related to sustainability. This crisis could cause significant, even devas-tating, problems for humankind in the future, before people finally find the will to make significant changes. One author, Paul Gilding, claims that a "great disruption" will be needed before people find the will to make necessary changes to avoid disastrous problems related to climate change and sustainability.[122] The shamans among us believe that change is possible to avoid this possibility, but only if many, many more of us act in constructive ways to make the systemic changes that are needed.

Some argue that we can combine these two terms, "development" and "sustainability," in the form of "sustainable development." The famous Brundltand Commission report of 1987, called *Our Common Future*, in fact, invented the term. "Sustainable development" carries the implication that growth and development can continue indefinitely, if only they are done more sustainably. But there is a very real sense in which "seers" like Gilding understand that "sustainable development" is a kind of oxymoron or paradoxical statement. The implication of sustainable development is that largely unfettered continuous growth in material goods and consumption of resources, not to mention population growth, can continue, though we humans may need to change our ways to reduce waste, recycle materials more often, and not place so many demands on the natural environment. Further, many people believe that somehow we humans will find a way, perhaps through technological means, to continue economic material and population growth past the ecological limits that humanity is already pushing.

Scholars at the Stockholm Resilience Centre have found that there are nine "planetary boundaries" that, if exceeded, can potentially cause grave problems for humanity.[123] These scholars believe that humanity is already pushing past three of these nine boundaries and may well be near or exceeding two of the others. And population on the planet, which is already pushing

ecological limits at around 7.4 billion people (having quadru-
pled since 1900), is expected to rise to somewhere between 9
and 11 billion by 2050. Resource demands in such a scenario
can only become more intense.

Further, Kate Raworth has argued that, in addition to staying
within planetary ecological boundaries, there are a set of social
conditions that can build what she calls a "safe and just space
for humanity."[124] She builds her "doughnut" model using the
nine planetary boundaries beyond which environmental degra-
dation means the planet cannot support humanity's needs on
the outside, and 11 social priorities identified by the world's
nations on the inside. These conditions include sufficient food,
clean water, income, education, resilience, voice, jobs, energy,
social equity, gender equality, and health for the world's human
population. Raworth's 11 indicators are aligned with the United
Nations' 17 Sustainable Development Goals (SDGs), published
in 2016. The SDGs focus on: eradicating poverty; an end to
hunger; good health; quality education; gender equality; clean
water and sanitation; renewable energy; decent work; innovation and infrastructure; reduced inequalities; sustainable cities
and communities; responsible consumption; climate action; life
below the water; life on land; and peace and justice—to be
achieved through (often multi-sector) partnerships for the goals
(the 17th goal).

The planetary boundary conditions, the social priorities outlined by the doughnut framework, and the SDGs combine to
provide a macro set of issues on which today's shamans can
reasonably focus their efforts to heal the world around them.
Each of the areas of the SDGs can be tackled locally within communities, at regional and national levels, and globally. Each of
us can potentially do something with respect to at least one of

these areas or in whatever area of life our particular our healing capacities draw us.

There is plenty of evidence to suggest that humanity faces a potential existential crisis today. That possibility calls to all of us to develop whatever shamanic gifts we have to heal those parts of the world that we can touch, where we can make positive changes. To the extent that business-as-usual represents our current materialistically oriented culture, the shaman can help us to see the problems embedded in our ways.

The ability to see and envision new possibilities and to help ourselves and others act on those possibilities is desperately needed today. That is why there is such a need for so many more of us to become shamans today. Only with the healing orientation toward the world, the ability to connect across boundaries, relationships, and institutions, and the sensemaking ability to reshape our narrative stories that are characteristic of the shaman can we move humanity towards this necessary transition, or transformation of the current world order.

Endnotes

Preface

1. Joseph Campbell, *The Hero with a Thousand Faces*. Novato, CA: New World Library, 2008.

Acknowledgments

2. *The Difference Makers: How Social and Institutional Entrepreneurs Created the Corporate Responsibility Movement*. Sheffield, UK: Greenleaf Publishing, 2008. *Intellectual Shamans: Management Academics Making a Difference*. Cambridge, UK: Cambridge University Press, 2014.

1. Healing the world: why shamanism?

3. These ideas were first developed in Waddock, *Intellectual Shamans*. See also, Peter J. Frost and Carolyn P. Egri, "The Shamanic Perspective on Organizational Change and Development," *Journal of Organizational Change Management*, 7(1) (1994): 7-23, and Caroly P. Egri and Peter J. Frost, "Shamanism and Change: Bringing Back the Magic in Organizational Transformation," *Research in Organizational Change and Development*, 4 (1991): 175-221.

4. James Lovelock used the term "Gaia" to describe Earth as a living system in multiple books, including *Gaia: A New Look at Life on Earth*. Oxford, UK: Oxford University Press, 1979; and calls attention to the planet's ills in *The Revenge of Gaia: Earth's Climate Crisis and the Fate*

of Humanity. New York: Basic Books, 2007, and *The Vanishing Face of Gaia: The Final Warning*. PublicAffairs, 2009.

5. Serge Kahili King defines the shaman as a healer of relationships in *Urban Shaman*. New York: Simon & Schuster, 2009.

6. See, e.g., Berthold Laufer, "Origin of the Word Shaman," *American Anthropologist*, New Series, 19(3) (1971): 361-371.

7. Thanks to Igor Gurkov who gave me this translation in personal communication, June 13, 2016.

8. Mircia Eliade, *Shamanism: Archaic Techniques of Ecstasy*. Trans. Willard R. Trask; Princeton, NJ: Princeton University Press, 1964 (originally published 1951).

9. See Waddock, *Intellectual Shamans*.

10. See Waddock, *The Difference Makers*.

11. Eliade, *Shamanism*.

12. Carl G. Jung, *The Archetypes and the Collective Unconscious* (No. 20). Princeton, NJ: Princeton University Press, 1981.

2. Shamans: world healers among us

13. Waddock, *The Difference Makers*.

14. Waddock, *Intellectual Shamans*: 154-155.

15. Edward N. Lorenze of MIT discussed the concept of the strange attractor without labelling it as such in "Deterministic Nonperiodic Flow," *Journal of the Atmospheric Sciences*, 20(2) (1963): 130-141. The actual term was coined by David Ruelle and Floris Takens in "On the Nature of Turbulence," *Communications in Mathematical Physics*, 20(3) (1971): 167-192.

16. John Myerson's books are (with Robert K. Greenebaum) *Riding the Spirit Wind: Stories of Shamanic Healing*. LifeArts Press, 2003; (with Judith Robbins) *Voices from the Other Side of the Couch: A Warrior's View of Shamanic Healing*. LifeArts Press, 2008; and (with Judith Robbins), *Death Grip on the Pommel: A Warrior's Journey to Grace*. LifeArts Press, 2012).

17. See, for example, Amit Goswami, *The Self-Aware Universe: How Consciousness Creates the Material World*. New York: Penguin, 1994.

18. For examples see, e.g., any of Alberto Villoldo's books, including *One Spirit Medicine: Ancient Ways to Ultimate Wellness*. Carlsbad, CA: HayHouse, 2015; King, *Urban Shaman*; Roger Walsh, *The World of Shamanism: New Views of an Ancient Tradition*. Woodbury, MN: Llewellyn Publications, 2014; Michael Harner, *The Way of the Shaman*. New York:

HarperOne, 1990; Evelyn C. Rysdyk and Sandra Ingerman, *Spirit Walking: A Course in Shamanic Power*. Newburyport, MA: Weiser Books, 2013.

3. Today's shaman's work: healing, connecting, sensemaking

19. Frost and Egri, "The Shamanic Perspective," and Egri and Frost, "Shamanism and Change."
20. King, *Urban Shaman*.
21. Peter Frost and Carolyn Egri implicitly recognized this aspect of shamanism in their work on shamans as organization development specialists. See Frost and Egri, "The Shamanic Perspective."
22. See, for example, J. Rockström, W.L. Steffen, K. Noone, Å. Persson, F.S. Chapin III, E. Lambin *et al.*, "Planetary Boundaries: Exploring the Safe Operating Space for Humanity." *Ecology & Society*, 14(2) (2009): 32, http://www.ecologyandsociety.org/vol14/iss2/art32; and W. Steffen, K. Richardson, J. Rockström, S.E. Cornell, I. Fetzer, E.M. Bennett, R. Biggs, S.R. Carpenter, W. de Vries, C.A. de Wit, C. Folke, D. Gerten, J. Heinke, G.M. Mace, L.M. Persson, V. Ramanathan, B. Teyers and S. Sorlin, "Planetary Boundaries: Guiding Human Development on a Changing Planet." *Science*, 347(6223) (February 2015): 1259855-1-1249855-10.
23. See note 3.
24. For example, see F. Capra and P.L. Luisi, *The Systems View of Life: A Unifying Vision*. Cambridge, UK: Cambridge University Press, 2014.
25. Wilber has written numerous books in which he discusses these ideas, including *The Fourth Turning: Imagining the Evolution of an Integral Buddhism*. Boston: Shambhala, 2014; *The Eye of Spirit: An Integral Vision for a World Gone Slightly Mad*. Boston: Shambhala, 1998; *Sex, Ecology, Spirituality: The Spirit of Evolution*. Boston: Shambhala, 1995; *The Marriage of Sense and Soul: Integrating Science and Reason*. New York: Random House, 1998; and *A Theory of Everything: An Integral Vision for Business, Politics, Science and Spirituality*. Boston: Shambhala, 2002. Perhaps the most relevant and accessible for the shamanic practitioner is *Integral Life Practice: A 21st Century Blueprint for Physical Health, Emotional Balance, Mental Clarity and Spiritual Awakening* by Wilber, Terry Patten, Adam Leonard, and Marco Morell (Integral Books, 2008).
26. See Wilber, *The Fourth Turning*: Loc 1854.
27. See, e.g., Mihály Csíkszentmihalyi, *Flow: The Psychology of Optimal Experience*. New York: Harper Perennial, 1991; *Creativity: Flow and*

the Psychology of Discovery and Invention. New York: HarperCollins, 1996; and *Finding Flow: The Psychology of Engagement with Everyday Life*. New York: Basic Books, 1997.

28. King, *Urban Shaman*.

29. Donna Hicks, *Dignity: The Essential Role It Plays in Resolving Conflict*. New Haven, CT: Yale University Press, 2011.

30. Jane Dutton, 2015 Lifetime Achievement Award Address, Academy of Management, Organizational Behavior Division, posted at: https://www.youtube.com/watch?v=CUamHuNkTk4.

31. The term "imaginal" was coined by Henri Corbin and R. Horine in *Mundus Imaginalis, or The Imaginary and the Imaginal*. Ipswich: Golgonooza Press, 1976.

32. One important reference is Karl E. Weick, *Sensemaking in Organizations*. Thousand Oaks, CA: Sage, 1995.

33. Brenda Dervin, "Sense-making Theory and Practice: An Overview of User Interest in Knowledge Seeking and Use." *Journal of Knowledge Management*, 2(2) (1998): 36-46 (42).

34. J. Dow, "Universal Aspects of Symbolic Healing: A Theoretical Synthesis." *American Anthropologist*, 88(1) (1986): 56-69.

35. Frost and Egri ("The Shamanic Perspective") term this function "spiritual leadership" as well as sensemaking.

36. See note 18 for details of Villoldo's many books.

37. D. Buettner, *The Blue Zones: Nine Lessons for Living Longer from the People Who've Lived the Longest*. National Geographic Books, 2012.

4. Answering your call to purpose

38. Reflecting Robert Frost's poem "The Road Less Travelled."

39. Joseph Campbell, *The Masks of God: Primitive Mythology*. Arkana, 1991.

40. George Leonard and Michael Murphy, *The Life We Are Given: A Long-Term Program for Realizing the Potential of Body, Mind, Heart and Soul*. New York: Jeremy P. Tarcher (Putnam), 1995.

41. Wilber *et al.*, *Integral Life Practice*.

42. Robert Kegan and Lisa Laskow Lahey, *An Everyone Culture: Becoming a Deliberately Developmental Organization*. Cambridge, MA: Harvard Business Review Press, 2016.

43. Perhaps a good place for Westerners without experience to start is with the work of Jon Kabat-Zinn, *Wherever You Go, There You Are: Mindfulness Meditation in Everyday Life*. New York: Hyperion, 1995; *Coming*

to *Our Senses: Healing Ourselves and the World through Mindfulness*. New York: Hyperion, 2005; and *Full Catastrophe Living (Revised Edition): Using the Wisdom of Your Body and Mind to Face Stress, Pain, and Illness*. New York: Bantam, 2013.

44. Csíkszentmihályi, *Flow*; *Creativity*; *Finding Flow*; and also *The Evolving Self: A Psychology for the Third Millennium*. New York: Harper Perennial, 1994.

45. E. Hatfield, J.T. Cacioppo, and R.L. Rapson, *Emotional Contagion*. Cambridge, UK: Cambridge University Press, 1994.

46. Frost and Egri, "The Shamanic Perspective."

47. Carl G. Jung, "The Concept of the Collective Unconscious." In *Collected Works*, 9(1) (1936): 42, posted at: http://www.bahaistudies.net/asma/The-Concept-of-the-Collective-Unconscious.pdf.

5. Balance and harmony in self and the world

48. King, *Urban Shaman*: 14.

49. See Frost and Egri, "The Shamanic Perspective", and Egri and Frost, "Shamanism and Change."

50. How the chess master experiences the chessboard differently from less experienced individuals was explored in depth years ago by Herbert Simon and written up (among other places) in H. Simon and W. Chase, "Skill in Chess." In *Computer Chess Compendium*. New York: Springer, 1988: 175-188.

51. See, for example, Csíkszentmihályi, *Flow*; *Creativity*; and *Finding Flow*.

52. Jung, "The Concept of the Collective Unconscious."

53. Capra and Luisi, *The Systems View of Life*: 276.

54. Abraham Maslow, *Toward a Psychology of Being*. Princeton, NJ: Van Nostrand, 1962.

55. Csíkszentmihályi, *Flow*.

56. Kabat-Zinn, *Wherever You Go, There You Are*.

57. Capra and Luisi, *The Systems View of Life*.

58. Capra and Luisi, *The Systems View of Life*: 278.

59. Capra and Luisi, *The Systems View of Life*: 278.

60. Albert Einstein, "The World as I See It" (1949). Posted at: http://www.emmanouela.yolasite.com/resources/The%20World%20As%20I%20See%20It%20-%20Einstein.pdf: 5.

61. www.theelders.org/about

62. Susan Blackmore, *The Meme Machine*. Oxford, UK: Oxford Paperbacks, 2000.

63. Sandra Waddock, "Finding Wisdom Within: The Role of Seeing and Reflective Practice in Developing Moral Imagination, Aesthetic Sensibility, and Systems Understanding." *Journal of Business Ethics Education,* 7 (2010): 177-196; and "Wisdom and Responsible Leadership: Aesthetic Sensibility, Moral Imagination, and Systems Thinking." In Daryl Koehn and Dawn Elm (Eds.), *Aesthetics and Business Ethics: Issues in Business Ethics,* Vol. 41. Netherlands: Springer, 2014: 129-147.

64. See Patricia Werhane, "Mental Models, Mental Models, Moral Imagination and System Thinking in the Age of Globalization." *Journal of Business Ethics,* 78 (2008): 463-474.

65. See, for example, Wilber, *The Fourth Turning.*

66. See, for example, Lovelock, *Gaia; The Revenge of Gaia;* and *The Vanishing Face of Gaia: A Final Warning.* New York: Basic Books, 2010.

67. See Goswami, *The Self-Aware Universe.*

68. See Fritjof Capra, *The Web of Life.* New York: Anchor Doubleday, 1995; "Complexity and Life." *Theory, Culture & Society,* 22(5) (2005): 33-44; and Capra and Luisi, *The Systems View of Life.*

69. See Capra and Luisi, *The Systems View of Life.*

70. H. Gardner, *Frames of Mind: The Theory of Multiple Intelligences.* New York: Basic Books, 2011. H. Gardner, *Intelligence Reframed: Multiple Intelligences for the 21st Century.* New York: Basic Books, 1999.

71. See Robert Kegan, *The Evolving Self: Problem and Process in Human Development.* Cambridge, MA: Harvard University Press, 1982, and *In Over Our Heads: The Mental Demands of Modern Life.* Cambridge, MA: Harvard University Press, 1994; William R. Torbert and associates, *Action Inquiry: The Secret of Timely and Transforming Leadership.* San Francisco: Berrett-Koehler, 2004; Ken Wilber, *Integral Spirituality: A Startling New Role for Religion in the Modern and Post-Modern World.* Boston, MA: Shambhala Publications, 2006; and *Sex, Ecology, Spirituality.*

72. Richard Dawkins, *The Selfish Gene.* London: Oxford University Press, 2006 (1976).

73. Blackmore, *The Meme Machine.*

74. John Perkins, *Shapeshifting: Techniques for Global and Personal Transformation.* Inner Traditions/Bear & Co., 1997.

75. Sandra Waddock, "Reflections: Intellectual Shamans, Sensemaking, and Memes in Large System Change." *Journal of Change Management,* 15(4) (2015): 259-273.

76. Capra, *The Web of Life.*

77. George Lakoff describes the "good father" authoritarian leader in *The All New Don't Think of an Elephant! Know Your Values and Frame the Debate*. White River Junction, VT: Chelsea Green Publishing, 2014.

78. Marianne Williamson, *A Return to Love*. New York: HarperCollins, 1992: 190.

79. Williamson, *A Return to Love*: 190.

6. Science, the shaman, and our world

80. See, e.g., *The Fourth Turning*; *Sex, Ecology, Spirituality*; *A Brief History of Everything*. Boston, MA: Shambhala Publications, 1996, and Wilber *et al.*, *Integral Life Practice*.

81. A group of us have explored these issue deeply in S. Waddock, D. Dentoni, G. Meszoely, and S. Waddell, "The Complexity of Wicked Problems in Large System Change." *Journal of Organizational Change Management*, 28(6) (2015): 993-1,012; and S. Waddell, S. Waddock, S. Cornell, D. Dentoni, M. McLachlan, and G. Meszoely, "Large System Change: An Emerging Field of Transformation and Transitions." *Journal of Corporate Citizenship*, 58 (June 2015): 5-30. And I have looked at the idea of memes in Waddock, "Reflections."

82. This quote is from a paper entitled "Intellectual Shamans, Wayfinders, and Edgewalkers: Academics and System Change," by Sandra Waddock, Malcolm McIntosh, Judith Neal, Edwina Pio, and Chellie Spiller, which is the Editors' Introduction to a special issue entitled "Intellectual Shamans, Wayfinders, Edgewalkers, and Systems Thinkers: Building a World Where All Can Thrive." *Journal of Corporate Citizenship*, 62 (June 2016): 5-10.

83. These ideas are explored in depth in, among other places, B. Rosenblum and F. Kuttner, *Quantum Enigma: Physics Encounters Consciousness*. Oxford, UK: Oxford University Press, 2011.

84. Joni Mitchell's song "Woodstock," inspired by the Woodstock festival of 1969, contains this sentiment.

85. See, for example, Bruce H. Lipton and Steve Bhaerman, *Spontaneous Evolution: Our Positive Future and How to Get There*. New York: Hay House, 2009.

86. Capra and Luisi, *The Systems View of Life*: 286.

87. See e.g. Wilber, *A Brief History of Everything*.

88. For example, see the work of Lawrence Kohlberg, "Stages and Aging in Moral Development: Some Speculation." *Gerontologists*, 1 (1973): 498-502; and "Moral Stages and Moralization: The Cognitive-Developmental

Approach." in Thomas Lickona (Ed.) and Gilbert Geis and Lawrence Kohlberg (consulting editors), *Moral Development and Behavior: Theory, Research, and Social Issues*. New York: Holt, Rinehart & Winston, 1976. Also, Carol Gilligan, *In a Different Voice: Psychological Theory and Women's Development*. Cambridge, MA: Harvard University Press, 1982; Kegan, *The Evolving Self* and *In Over Our Heads*; and Torbert, *Action Inquiry*.

89. Wilber, *The Fourth Turning*.

90. Wilber, *The Fourth Turning*.

91. Clare W. Graves, "Levels of Existence: An Open System Theory of Values." *Journal of Humanistic Psychology*, 10(2) (1970): 131-155; and "Human Nature Prepares for a Momentous Leap." *The Futurist*, 8(2) (1974): 72-85. See also Don Edward Beck and Christopher C. Cowan, *Spiral Dynamics: Mastering Values, Leadership and Change*. Hoboken, NJ: Wiley-Blackwell, 2005, who translated Graves's work into what they called "spiral dynamics."

92. Kegan, *In Over Our Heads*.

93. Capra and Luisi, *The Systems View of Life*.

94. F. Capra and P.L. Luisi, *The Systems View of Life: A Unifying Vision*. Cambridge University Press, 2014.

95. See http://www.mcescher.com/gallery/most-popular/drawing-hands for an image.

96. See http://www.mcescher.com/gallery/back-in-holland/relativity.

97. See http://www.mcescher.com/gallery/recognition-success/ascending-and-descending.

98. Robert Perey, "Organizing Sustainability and the Problem of Scale: Local, Global, or Fractal?" *Organization & Environment*, 27(3) (2014): 215-222.

99. See also Waddock, "Reflections"; and "Foundational Memes for a New Narrative about the Role of Business in Society." *Humanistic Management Journal*, online 2016, DOI: 10.1007/s41463-016-0012-4.

100. For two analyses, see John Ehrenfeld and Andrew Hoffman, *Flourishing: A Frank Conversation about Sustainability*. Palo Alto, CA: Stanford, 2013; and Tim Jackson, *Prosperity without Growth: Economics for a Finite Planet*. Abington, UK: Routledge, 2011.

101. E.g. Blackmore, *The Meme Machine*.

102. Perey, "Organizing Sustainability and the Problem of Scale": 220.

103. There are many sources for these ideas, among them James Gleick, *Chaos: Making a New Science*. New York: Viking, 1987; Gary M. Grobman,

"Complexity Theory: A New Way to Look at Organizational Change." *Public Administration Quarterly*, 2005, 350-382; S. Kauffman, *At Home in the Universe: The Search for the Laws of Self-Organization and Complexity*. New York: Oxford University Press, 1995; M.R. Lissack and H. Letiche, "Complexity, Emergence, Resilience, and Coherence: Gaining Perspective on Organizations and their Study." Emergence, 4(3) (2002): 72–94; Nicolis Gregoire and Ilya Priggine, *Exploring Complexity: An Introduction*. New York: W.H. Freeman, 1989; I. Prigogine and I. Stengers, *Order Out of Chaos: Man's New Dialogue with Nature*. Boulder, CO: New Science Library, 1984.

104. Lovelock, *Gaia*; *The Revenge of Gaia*; and *The Vanishing Face of Gaia*.

105. Edward N. Lorenz, "Atmospheric Predictability as Revealed by Naturally Occurring Analogues." *Journal of the Atmospheric Sciences*, 26(4) (1969): 636-646.

106. Otto Scharmer, *Leading from the Emerging Future: From Ego-system to Eco-system Economies*. San Francisco: Berrett-Koehler, 2013.

107. J. Dow, "Universal Aspects of Symbolic Healing: A Theoretical Synthesis." *American Anthropologist*, 88(1) (1986): 56-69.

7. The shaman as leader today

108. Malcolm McIntosh (Ed.), *The Necessary Transition: The Journey towards the Sustainable Enterprise Economy*. Sheffield, UK: Greenleaf Publishing, 2013.

109. Blackmore, *The Meme Machine*.

110. Waddock, "Reflections."

111. For more detailed analysis, see Waddock, "Foundational Memes for a New Narrative."

112. These ideas are drawn from Blackmore, *The Meme Machine*, and further developed in the context of system change in Waddock, "Reflections."

113. See Blackmore, *The Meme Machine*.

114. Waddock, "Reflections."

115. Jon Ronson, *The Psychopath Test: A Journey through the Madness Industry*. Riverhead Books, 2012.

116. See Hicks, *Dignity*, for an elaboration of the concept of dignity and its differentiation from respect.

117. Thomas Donaldson and James P. Walsh, "Toward a Theory of Business." *Research in Organizational Behavior*, 35 (2015): 181-207.

118. Eric Schlosser, *Fast Food Nation: The Dark Side of the All-American Meal*. Boston, MA: Houghton Mifflin Harcourt, 2012.

119. Michael Pollan, *The Omnivore's Dilemma: A Natural History of Four Meals*. New York: Penguin, 2006.

120. Collective value as per Donaldson and Walsh, "Toward a Theory of Business"; and wellbeing and dignity as stated by the Humanistic Management Network and Leading for Wellbeing Initiatives: http://www.humanetwork.org, http://natcapsolutions.org/leading-for-wellbeing, and https://weatherhead.case.edu/news/2016/02/11/leading-for-well-being.

121. W. McDonough and M. Braungart, *Cradle to Cradle: Remaking the Way we Make Things*. New York: Macmillan, 2010.

122. Paul Gilding, *The Great Disruption: How the Climate Crisis will Transform the Global Economy*. Bloomsbury Publishing, 2011.

123. Rockström *et al.*, "Planetary Boundaries"; L.M. Persson, V. Ramanathan, B. Teyers, and S. Sorlin, "Planetary Boundaries: Guiding Human Development on a Changing Planet." *Science*, 347(6223) (February 2015): 1259855-1-1249855-10.

124. Kate Raworth, "A Safe and Just Space for Humanity: Can we Live within the Doughnut?" *Oxfam Policy and Practice: Climate Change and Resilience*, 8(1) (2012): 1-26.

For Product Safety Concerns and Information please contact our EU
representative GPSR@taylorandfrancis.com
Taylor & Francis Verlag GmbH, Kaufingerstraße 24, 80331 München, Germany